Speaking Skills for Business Careers

Speaking Skills for Business Careers

Dennis Becker, President

Paula Borkum Becker, Vice President of Corporate Affairs
The Speech Improvement Company, Inc.

GLENCOE
McGraw-Hill

New York, New York   Columbus, Ohio   Woodland Hills, California   Peoria, Illinois

Library of Congress Cataloging-in-Publication Data

Becker, Dennis

    Speaking skills for business careers / Dennis Becker, Paula Borkum Becker.

      p.   cm.

    ISBN 0-256-12630-5

    1. Business communication.   2. Business presentation.   3. Public

speaking. I. Becker, Dennis, date. II. Title.

HF5718.B43   1993

658.4′52 — dc20   92–27382

Send all inquiries to:
Glencoe/McGraw-Hill
21600 Oxnard St., Suite 500
Woodland Hills, CA 91367-4906

Printed in the United States of America.
  8 9 10   071   03 02

Preface

Speaking is such a natural, common experience that few people ever stop to think about it. In the business world this can be costly. Technical misrepresentations, poor first impressions, and ineffective speaking styles can hurt your career. *Speaking Skills for Business Careers* offers practical guidance on building speaking confidence and enhancing speaking effectiveness in the business environment. Skill in speaking is necessary at all career stages — from the employment interview, to daily job performance, to job advancement. Career success depends on making the most of every speaking opportunity from the most casual to the most formal. Once you've mastered *Speaking Skills for Business Careers,* you'll be well on your way to getting and keeping the job you want.

This is a *practical* book based on the speaking experiences of business professionals. Therefore, we have focused on 10 skills most crucial to successful business speaking:

- Controlling the Fear of Speaking
- Speaking Clearly
- Preparing and Organizing
- Informing and Persuading
- Participating in Meetings
- Choosing Effective Language
- Mastering Nonverbal Communication
- Learning to Listen
- Using the Telephone
- Using Visual Aids

These are *the* speaking skills needed in the world of work. *Speaking Skills for Business Careers* provides tools to master these skills. These are concrete and realistic techniques to build on existing speaking strengths and help develop new ones.

After years of instructing students and coaching business professionals, we have found that the best way to learn any set of skills is to understand how they are used in context, and practice them accordingly. Therefore, this book focuses on business situations where effective speaking is essential. The explanations and examples in the text are geared toward business settings: controlling nervousness, handling telephone communications, speaking informatively and persuasively, developing brief presentations, getting the most out of meetings, developing listening skills, and mastering visual aids. This book covers every type of speaking that is called for on the job. These are practical skills needed for business careers.

We have used nontechnical language throughout the book to cover *all* topics, including the communication process, speech organization techniques, voice quality, and language choice. In-text teaching features underscore the direct, practical approach of *Speaking Skills for Business Careers:*

Chapter Objectives open each chapter with a list of objectives which identify the most important chapter themes and skills. These objectives guide students toward a common goal of understanding and also provide a brief preview of the chapter's main concepts. Implicit in these objectives are personal and business benefits of each chapter.

Exercises at the end of each chapter show students how to put speaking skills into practice. These are active skill-oriented exercises which can be completed in class teams or as homework assignments. Students are encouraged to hone their business speaking skills in realistic business settings.

Quick Quizzes test student comprehension of chapter highlights. These quizzes serve as instant self-checks on chapter comprehension. They can be completed in class or for homework.

The *Instructor's Resource Manual* offers answers to text Quick Quizzes, chapter outlines, brief teaching suggestions, transparency masters, and a bibliography.

Acknowledgments

We would like to acknowledge the reviewers who read and commented on the manuscript throughout its development. Their assistance and support was invaluable:

Anita Brownstein,
Drake Business School,
New York, NY

Marilyn Chernoff,
Sawyer School,
Pittsburgh, PA

Pat DeBold,
Concorde Career Colleges,
Kansas City, MO

Vincent Miskell,
Metropolitan Career Institute,
New York, NY

Dorothy Moore,
Fort Lauderdale College,
Fort Lauderdale, FL

Jo Anne Mount,
Bradford School,
Pittsburgh, PA

Jack Perella,
Santa Rosa Junior College,
Santa Rosa, CA

Jean Perry,
Glendale College,
Glendale, CA

Phyllis Riley,
South Hills Business School,
State College, PA

Marlene Stys,
Barnes Business College,
Denver, CO

Colleen Switala,
Bryant & Stratton Business Institute,
Buffalo, NY

The materials, techniques, and exercises in this text have been developed by staff members at The Speech Improvement Co. in Boston. We are grateful to them for permitting their use. In addition, we'd like to thank the many business professionals whose daily speaking experiences provided the basis for this text.

Please feel free to contact us directly with any questions or concerns about this text. Our office is located at

The Speech Improvement Company, Inc.
1614 Beacon St.
Boston (Brookline), MA 02146
1-800-LETS-RAP

Dennis Becker Ph.D.
Paula Borkum Becker Ph.D.

About the Authors

Paula Borkum Becker and Dennis Becker are co-founders of The Speech Improvement Company, Inc. Since 1964 this Boston-based firm has specialized in communication training with a focus on business speaking. The Beckers' nationwide client base includes major corporations and start-up businesses, giving them combined expertise in all areas of business speaking. Both authors are experienced instructors and speech coaches in business settings and in the classroom. The text's techniques and exercises are drawn from these resources.

Contents

Communication and Business Speaking

"Delivering a message clearly, concisely and in a manner that leaves little doubt of your intent is the first responsibility of sound management; it's your job!"
Stan Hirschman, *Vice-president, Store Operations, Software, Etc.*

Chapter Objectives

After reading this chapter you will be able to:

1. Identify the most important business-speaking skills.
2. Develop a positive attitude toward business speaking.
3. Understand the components of the communication process.
4. Plan appropriate speaking strategies for different situations.

Business speaking is a form of communication used to conduct business. Communication is the exchange of ideas between people. The key word is *exchange*. This is especially true in business speaking. In business, effective communication takes place when there is enough common understanding that an exchange of ideas can take place.

Figure 1–1 illustrates the four components necessary to the flow of communication: speaker (or sender), message (the ideas exchanged), channel (the means of communication such as speech, writing, or pictures), and listener (or receiver). You'll see these components again when we discuss the Silver Square of communication. Each of these four components uses techniques that will be addressed in this book. Chapter 1 will introduce you to some of these techniques and topics, which will be considered in greater detail in subsequent chapters.

Nonbusiness speaking also involves these components, but it may not affect anyone other than the actual participants in the communication—speaker and listener. Business speaking, however, frequently has a direct effect on many other people. In fact, it may have a direct impact on your job. Therefore, it's wise to be aware of and in control of all the components and techniques related to the communication process. The more you understand the process, the better business speaker you'll be, and that is directly linked to your career success.

In this chapter, we define business speaking. We will review the three most common business-speaking situations and the skills needed for success. These skills will be broken down into step-by-step explanations in later chapters.

Business-Speaking Environments

Your business career will bring you in contact with several communication mediums including telephones, fax machines, video conferencing, memos, computers, and annual reports. However, the most common and most important communication tool is *speaking*. In the business world, you'll be speaking from 9 A.M. to 5 P.M. and beyond, all day, and every day. The three most common business-speaking environments are (1) one-on-one meetings, (2) group meetings, and (3) presentations.

FIGURE 1–1

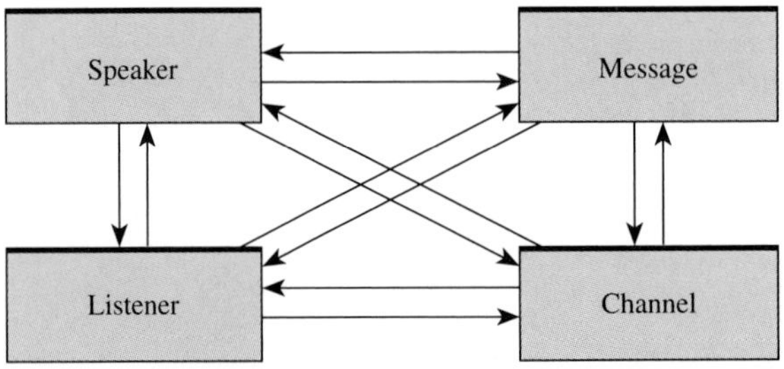

One-on-One Meetings

Dozens or even hundreds of times daily and weekly, you will speak with another person about a business issue. It may be a simple question-and answer encounter, a simple greeting, or a more formal experience such as an interview, performance appraisal, or training session. These one-on-one speaking situations will be either face-to-face or over the telephone, often impromptu, and unprepared. They may be initiated by you, a colleague, a supervisor, a customer or client, or many other people. Some examples of one-on-one dialogue follow:

> "Hey, Greg, what was the outcome of the meeting yesterday?"
> "Well, we agreed to initiate three new procedures. I'll stop by your office right after lunch to review them."
>
> "Molly tells me that I should ask you for the update on the project. First of all, is that correct? And then how should we do that?"
> "Yes, I'll be glad to update you. Let me know if you'd like a written or oral report."
>
> "I don't really understand this new phone system."
> "Neither do I, but I've used it enough to at least tell you how to make calls. Would it be helpful if I go over that with you?"

Group Meetings

In addition to one-on-one speaking experiences, group meetings are the next most common speaking situation. Group meetings are encounters between two or more people. The list of meetings you attend is nearly endless. It may include:

Brainstorming.	Workshops.
Quality control.	Budget.
Debriefings.	Training.
Staff conferences.	Board.
Marketing and sales.	Community.
Seminars.	Department.
Negotiating.	Problem solving.

The start of a group meeting might sound something like this:

> "I'd like to get this meeting started by saying that we have two items on the agenda. The first is, 'How should we control smoking during work hours in the building?' The second is, 'What suggestions do you have for office coverage during the upcoming holiday season?' We'll discuss each for approximately 15 minutes. Any questions before we start?"
> "Yes, what will be done with the answers to these questions?"
> "I have a question, too. May we take a break between topics?"

Presentations

Presentations, familiar to most business professionals, are an accepted form of communication and can be formal or informal. Most commonly, they are formal. Group presentations can occur in any of the one-on-one or group meetings situations just described. Presentations are an excellent opportunity for you to highlight your knowledge and understanding of a subject and to show your insight, creativity, style, and enthusiasm.

> "Good morning. This morning I'll be speaking for approximately 10 minutes on the topic of quality assurance measures. I'll be emphasizing three points: (1) the company definition of quality assurance, (2) the measures already in place, and (3) new measures we'll be introducing. This should be valuable information to each of you because it will prepare you for the new emphasis on quality assurance and ensure a less stressful integration of the new measurement into your daily routine."

Business-Speaking Skills

The following 10 business-speaking skills are called on most frequently by successful business speakers.

1. Controlling the Fear of Speaking

The fear of speaking has interfered with and prevented the successful growth and development of more business careers than any other single factor. It strikes at all levels, ages, business disciplines, and both sexes. The saddest part is that it doesn't have to happen. *You can learn to understand and control the fear of speaking*. In Chapter 2, we will help you to do just that.

2. Speaking Clearly

Speech discrimination is very real. We all practice it. That is, we judge people by the way they speak. What's your impression of people who say, "deez, dem, doz," rather than "these, them, those"? It may not be fair, but people do draw conclusions about you by the way you speak. Speaking clearly means controlling articulation, pronunciation, speed, and vocal variety. All this ensures that you will be an intelligible and interesting speaker. In Chapter 3, we will provide specific techniques and exercises to strengthen these skills.

3. Prepare and Organize for Business Speaking

Organization may be the most distinguishing factor separating business speaking from all other speaking. In social conversation, people frequently switch subjects or start and stop in the middle of a thought. In business speaking, however, you are expected to be well organized. In Chapter 4, we will provide you with two practical organizational tools so you can understand how other people organize and how you can improve your own organization.

4. Informing and Persuading

Some business speaking is 90 percent giving information and 10 percent persuading your listeners to accept it, whereas other business speaking is 10 percent giving information and 90 percent persuading your listeners to accept it. Convincing people to do what you would like them to do is a positive business-speaking skill. Although persuasion can occur in many ways, in Chapter 5 we will provide you with the three best methods of persuasion.

5. Participating in Meetings

As we mentioned earlier, meetings are among the most common settings for business speaking. In Chapter 6, we will cover meeting types, behaviors, and processes. We will also present techniques that can help you when you interview to get a job or to give a job, including the five-point self-sell outline.

6. Language and Word Choice

Business speaking, of course, is not just how you organize, present, and deliver your speech. The basic elements of your speech, the words you choose, have a major impact on the effectiveness of your speech. In Chapter 7 "Language and Word Choice," we'll cover the basics of how to choose just the right word to fit particular business speaking situations. Since business settings vary from formal to informal, and purposes vary from information, to problem solving, to persuasion, you'll need to know how to tailor your word choice to fit different settings and purposes.

7. Nonverbal Communication

The term *business speaking* normally implies direct human speech. However, often more than half of what you communicate is nonverbal. The way you move and your appearance are all forms of nonverbal communication. In Chapter 8 we will cover nonverbal communication for the business environment.

8. Learning to Listen

Most effective business speakers agree that to be an effective speaker, you must also be an effective listener. Listening well is not something that just happens—you can learn to improve your listening skills, which in turn will help improve your business-speaking skills. In Chapter 9 we will provide you with five guidelines for effective listening.

9. *Effective Telephone Skills*

The telephone is probably the most common and perhaps the most effective business tool you will ever use. Despite this truism, few business professionals ever learn how to use the telephone effectively. In Chapter 10 we will provide you with tips and techniques for effective telephone use, including some suggestions on using voice mail.

10. *Using Visual Aids*

Business speakers regularly use visual materials to clarify and emphasize. There is no doubt that some listeners learn better and are more persuaded by such visual materials as transparencies, 35 mm slides, flip charts, and handouts. These aids must be integrated into the speech in a smooth and comfortable manner. In Chapter 11, we will teach you the three most important guidelines for using visuals during business speaking.

Speaking Attitude: Be Positive

What is a speaking attitude? It is the way you *think* about the way you *speak*. It is what you believe about the value of speaking clearly, being organized, using visuals, being persuasive, listening, and controlling nonverbal behavior. If, for example, you think these things are not important, you are likely to be seen and heard as careless, sloppy, and even unintelligent. If you mumble and allow your thoughts to wander, you will appear self-centered and unpredictable. If, on the other hand, you have a strong, positive attitude about the impression you want to make on other people, you will learn the speaking skills discussed in this book and consider them as valuable as your other technical skills. Among other things, having a positive speaking attitude means:

- Being self-critical.
- Being enthusiastic about speaking opportunities.
- Being willing and able to adapt techniques to situations.
- Being willing to dedicate time to learn and practice, as you would with any other business skill.

Don't say, "That's the way I talk; I've been talking this way all my life. No one ever complained before." Take control of your business speaking by developing a positive attitude. Don't let yourself be a victim of negative thinking.

Speaking Enthusiasm

Enthusiasm is a positive characteristic that helps both speaker and listener. Enthusiasm is a general feeling of excitement about a subject. The word *enthusiasm* comes from the root words *en theos*, meaning in God. To us, the *IASM* at the end of the word has its own meaning:

I Am Sold Myself

Chapter Review

- The communication process consists of four major components:
  1. Speaker.
  2. Message.
  3. Channel.
  4. Listener.
- Most business speaking takes place in one of these three settings:
  1. One-on-one meetings.
  2. Group meetings.
  3. Presentations.
- Approach business speaking with a positive attitude based on knowledge and understanding of the most important elements of effective business speaking.
- In business speaking, the 10 basic skills you'll use over and over are:
  1. Controlling the fear of speaking.
  2. Speaking clearly.
  3. Preparing and organizing for business speaking.
  4. Informing and persuading.
  5. Participating in meetings.
  6. Mastering language and word choice.
  7. Nonverbal communication.
  8. Learning to listen.
  9. Effective telephone skills.
  10. Using visual aids.
- Mastering these skills will lead to success in business speaking and, ultimately, to success in business.

Quick Quiz

1. What are the four components of the communication process?
2. What is the most common communication tool?
3. What are the three most common settings for business speaking?

4. Describe at least eight types of group meetings.

5. Why would a business presentation be an excellent opportunity to highlight your knowledge, understanding, insight, style, and enthusiasm?

6. What are the 10 most important skills to improve business speaking?

7. What single element has interfered with the growth and development of more business careers?

8. What is a speaking attitude?

9. What positive speaking characteristic helps both speaker and listener?

10. What can the *IASM* in the word *enthusiasm* mean?

Controlling the Fear
of Speaking

"Practice, practice, practice with feedback, feedback, feedback. Guided practice is what makes presentations exceptional, not practice alone. Professionals make it sound and look easy because of their intensive preparation. Practice before many people and ask what is being done right and what needs improvement."
Richard Skinner, DTM, *Past International President, Toastmasters International*

Chapter Objectives

After reading this chapter, you will be able to:

1. Define the fear of speaking.
2. Understand how controlling speaking fear can affect business speaking.
3. Identify the causes of speaking fear.
4. Develop techniques for controlling the fear of speaking.

One of the most important business speaking skills you'll ever learn is how to control the *fear of speaking*. Without this skill you'll find it extremely difficult to master any of the other business speaking skills. In this chapter, we'll define speaking fear and describe the effect this fear could have on your career.

Take a minute to assess your own feelings about speaking. Fill in your responses to the Fear of Speaking checklist. If you have more yes responses than no responses, you're in the same boat as most of your classmates and most beginning business speakers.

Fear of Speaking Checklist

In this checklist there are statements concerning your communications in a number of situations. Which response seems most appropriate for you? There are no right or wrong answers.

	Frequently	Sometimes	Never
1. I avoid speaking in front of groups whenever possible.			
2. My hands shake when I speak in front of groups.			
3. My body feels tense and uncomfortable while speaking in front of groups.			
4. I feel out of touch with reality when speaking in front of groups.			
5. I have many negative thoughts about speaking in front of a group.			
6. I feel physically uncomfortable before speaking in front of a group.			
7. My thoughts become confused while speaking in front of groups.			
8. I am nervous when certain people, such as authority figures, are listening to me.			
9. I feel nervous when speaking in group discussions.			
10. I am nervous when speaking to the media.			
11. I am nervous when asked unexpectedly to answer a question or give an opinion.			
12. I am nervous while speaking during a business phone call.			
13. I am nervous when speaking with people I do not know.			
14. I am nervous in social conversation.			
15. I am too nervous to speak without written support.			

What Is Fear of Speaking?

So many of us have experienced fear of speaking that each of us could provide a definition of it, and most of the answers would probably be very similar. For some, fear of speaking involves:

Sweaty palms.	Breaking out in a rash.
Vomiting.	Shaking knees.
Shortness of breath.	Blanking out.
Fainting.	Butterflies in the stomach.
Cracking voice.	Rapid pulse.

For still others, fear of speaking includes forgetting, fear of rejection, and poor self-image. There is truth in all these answers, and to a greater or lesser degree, almost all of us have experienced at least some of them.

The words used in the preceding list are actual symptoms of speaking fear. They are the end result of the fear and the confirmation that it exists. As an actual definition, we propose the following: Speaking fear is the real or perceived danger of personal or professional harm as the result of speaking, resulting in a diminished capacity to function. This definition, which is used in our offices, has been constructed after years of study and practical experience in helping people from all walks of life to understand and control their fear of speaking.

What Causes Speaking Fear?

Four major causes of speaking fear are: (1) caring adults, (2) early school experiences, (3) too much television, and (4) the actual event of speaking before a group.

1. Caring Adults

Many people feel that it was their parents or other adults telling them that they should be seen and not heard, and that children should not contribute to conversation, that created their initial fear of speaking. Although adults may not have realized it, their urge to raise a ''polite'' child may also have led to an adult who is afraid to speak.

2. School

Fearful adult speakers may also have taken cues from their early teachers. Because teachers are in such a powerful position, they have constant opportunities to influence speaking fear. Because teachers are role models and authority figures, their own speaking behavior may have a strong influence on the speaking behavior and attitude of their students. If a teacher exhibits a fear of speaking, that teacher's students may perceive that this behavior and attitude is appropriate and may internalize it.

We are convinced that the fear of speaking increases when teachers say things such as, ''Don't speak until I call on you,'' ''You're out of order,'' ''Wait your turn,'' and ''If you have something to say, come up to the front of the room and say it to everyone.''

3. Television

It is well known that children are highly teachable and impressionable through television. There have been accusations, charges, and counter-charges about the effect of television on children. Now, we add new condemnation: Television can also promote fear of speaking.

We emulate our television heroes:

- We try to dress like them.
- We try to act like them.
- We want to drive cars like them.
- We want to live like them.
- We even try to speak like them.

This is where we get into trouble. Clothes, cars, and conduct may be relatively easy to reproduce, but speech is different. Our favorite television characters are not thinking on their own. They are not reacting spontaneously. They are repeating words written by someone else, words that they have rehearsed and refined. They are reacting to cues and timing. In short, they are not real. Intellectually, we know they are actors in a play, a movie, or a situation comedy. Intellectually, we understand that they are working with scenes, scripts, and sets. The problem, of course, is that we do not watch television intellectually—we watch it emotionally. We think we should be able to speak as well as the actors do. Using television characters as role models may inadvertently contribute to speaking fear.

4. The Speaking Event

For many people, even the *thought* of speaking before a group can take on a life of its own. These people are so terrified of speaking that they begin to exhibit the common signs of speaking fear, particularly the general nervousness and anxiety, even at the mere suggestion of making a speech. It's almost as if these people create the anxious feelings because they are so convinced that anxiety must always accompany speaking. However, they *can* anticipate these fears, control them, and short-circuit them before they grow out of proportion to the event. After practice, the word *speech* will no longer be charged with anxiety and fear.

Control Technique: The Silver Square

We call our technique for reducing fear the Silver Square. It has four sides, each one as valuable as the other three. When you are faced with a speaking opportunity that would normally create fear, prepare yourself in these four equally important areas:

1. Know yourself.
2. Know the topic.

The Silver Square

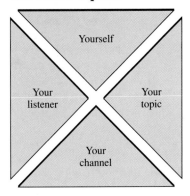

3. Know your listener.
4. Know your channel.

Speaking fear has both psychological and physiological components. Psychologically, it controls you with negative thoughts:

> "This is going to be awful."
> "I'm no good at this stuff."
> "I just know something will go wrong."
> "Everybody will think I'm so stupid."

Speaking fear also controls you by stimulating negative feelings.

> "If I fail at this, my job is on the line."
> "I'll bet they are out to see me make a fool of myself."
> "These slides are not good enough."
> "I don't know how to use a microphone."

People develop these negative thoughts days or weeks ahead of time and experience them throughout and after the speaking event. Such thoughts and reinforcing negative self-talk are very powerful and are among speaking fear's most harmful effects. "If you think you can, or if you think you can't, you're right."

Physiologically, fear of speaking controls you by:

• Putting a crack in your voice.
• Bringing on shaking hands or knees.
• Releasing butterflies in your stomach.
• Nearly choking off your breathing.

In more extreme cases, some people experience:

• Rashes.
• Fainting.

- Blind spots.
- Diarrhea.
- Vomiting.
- Sleeplessness.

The techniques of the Silver Square are designed to address psychological and physiological symptoms of the fear of speaking. Let's take a closer look at the four sides of the Silver Square.

Side 1: Know Yourself

- Do you have clear speech?
- Can you be understood easily?
- Is your voice loud or soft?
- Is your voice deep, tight, or squeaky?
- Do you speak fast or slowly?
- What facial expressions do you use?
- Do you like to speak with people?
- What types of people make you uncomfortable?
- What situations bring on nervousness?

Asking yourself these questions will provide valuable information about the way you handle speaking situations. Your answers are called *self-talk*.

Psychologically, it is important to control your self-talk. Speak positively. You will know that your positive self-talk is true when you are able to *exhibit* the speaking skill. The following are a few examples of how to turn negative self-talk into positive self-talk.

Negative	Positive
I just know something will go wrong.	I'm in control and can handle the unexpected.
Everyone will think I'm stupid.	My listeners will believe I know my material.
If I fail at this, my job is on the line.	This could be the beginning of real advancement for me.
I'll bet they are out to see me make a fool of myself.	Audiences don't want to be bored; they're on my side.
These slides aren't good enough.	My visuals clarify and emphasize my materials very well.

The Body Connection

Negative self-talk and negative attitudes can lead to physical signs of nervousness including a cracking voice, shaky knees, trembling hands, perspiring, and a jittery stomach. In turn, these unpleasant physical symptoms can be controlled by monitoring your breathing.

There are three types of breathing that we control. If you can learn to control your breathing, you can virtually eliminate the physical symptoms of your speaking fear.

The three types of breathing are:

1. *Clavicular* breathing: Used by an athlete who has completed a vigorous workout. It is panting, heavy breathing that gets its name from the movement of the clavicles (shoulder muscles) and the effort to inhale and exhale quickly. It is appropriate breathing for vigorous exercises, but not for speaking.

2. *Upper-thoracic* breathing: Used by a weight lifter about to lift a 300-pound barbell. He fills his chest (thorax) with air to increase the pressure and lifting capacity of his upper-thoracic muscles. Upper-thoracic breathing is appropriate breathing for lifting, pulling, throwing, and other upper body activities, but not for speaking.

3. *Diaphragmatic* breathing: Designed for the normal inhalation and exhalation process. It is controlled by the diaphragm, a huge dome-shaped muscle just below the rib cage (see Figure 2–1). Because it is the body's natural method of breathing, diaphragmatic breathing is instrumental in natural childbirth, yoga exercises, singing lessons, and many other control and relaxation situations. *It is also the most appropriate breathing for speaking.*

FIGURE 2–1 **The Human Breathing/Speaking System**

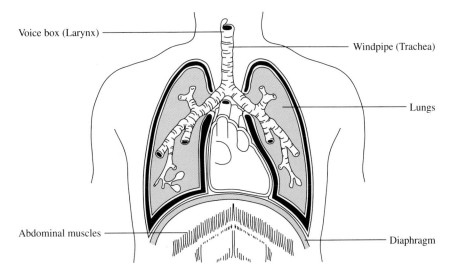

Voice box (Larynx)

Windpipe (Trachea)

Lungs

Abdominal muscles

Diaphragm

The next time nervous symptoms start to appear, check your breathing. Have you switched from diaphragmatic to upper-thoracic breathing? Trembling hands, knees, cheeks, lips, or anything else are direct results of pressure buildup from upper-thoracic breathing.

What can be done about this? Can it be controlled? What if you breathe upper-thoracically all the time? Is there any hope? Here is an easy and helpful exercise that produces quick results. Read it all the way through before you attempt it yourself.

Diaphragmatic Breathing Exercise

As you inhale, the diaphragm moves down and pushes out slightly. This allows the lungs to extend and fill with air. After a second or two, when the body has processed the inhaled air, the diaphragm pushes back up and compresses the air out of the lungs in exhalation. This process continues throughout life. When you breath *in,* the diaphragm goes *out.* When you breathe *out,* the diaphragm goes *in.*

1. Sit or stand comfortably in front of a mirror, so you can observe the process.
2. Use your fingertips to push lightly on your diaphragm, located just below your rib cage. Feel the movement as you breathe.
3. Inhale slowly through the nose or mouth. Feel the diaphragm push out. The shoulders and the upper chest should not move.
4. Hold this inhalation for three seconds.
5. As you exhale, try to count up to 20 by saying, ''one by one, two by two, three by three,'' and so on until you reach 20).
6. Stop when exhalation becomes a strain or you feel dizzy.
7. If you do not reach 20 on one breath, repeat this exercise 10 times. Do this three times daily until you can do 20 repetitions comfortably.

At first, you may experience some difficulty in doing this exercise. Diaphragmatic breathing is so familiar that it feels unnatural to concentrate on it. Yet, concentration is exactly what is needed to prevent the switch from diaphragmatic breathing to upper-thoracic breathing that occurs with nervousness. Knowing your feelings about speaking, identifying your negative self-talk, and focusing on proper breathing can all work toward conquering your speaking fears.

Side 2: Know Your Topic

The second side of the Silver Square is Know Your Topic. You may be able to recall several people talking at great length about subjects they knew little or nothing about. Or you've heard people who knew so much—except when to stop.

Knowing your topic means being aware of what you know and what you don't know. Many speakers say things like, ''What if I leave out something important?'' Or, ''I'm afraid they might ask me something I don't know.'' Remember, you are not a machine that can be programmed precisely for all contingencies. Worrying about them won't help. Being aware of what you know and don't know about your topic *will*. Remember, audiences don't want you to fail. They don't want you to look or feel stupid. If you do a poor job, they lose. They waste their time. No one *hopes* to sit through a dull, boring, meaningless speech. Your listeners are actually rooting for you *and* for themselves.

Knowing your topic also means knowing whether your speech is intended to be informative, persuasive, educational, or inspirational, or if it combines these purposes.

In business speaking, the purpose for speaking is usually clear. You may be part of a problem-solving meeting, a brainstorming session, or another meeting with a stated purpose. In some cases, you may be asked by your boss to give a progress report on a project. If you are not sure what the purpose of your speaking is, just ask what is expected of you—don't be shy. Asking for information before you attend a meeting will not be seen as a weakness. In fact, you will be admired for your conscientious efforts to be prepared. For your part, you'll feel much more comfortable and confident that you have identified any weak points in your understanding of the topic. It will give you a chance to research or prepare appropriately before your speaking opportunity.

Knowing your topic means knowing your own biases, strengths, and weaknesses concerning the topic. Be honest and critical with yourself about areas of the topic that are very familiar, those that are vaguely familiar, and those with which you are totally unfamiliar. Although you may conclude that what you don't know is a weakness, remember that this realization is a real strength—you won't be caught off guard in unfamiliar areas and you can plan your speech and strategy around both your strengths and weaknesses.

Side 3: Know Your Listener

The third side of the Silver Square is Know Your Listener. Almost everyone is a little apprehensive about facing a new situation, experience, or listener. In a business-speaking situation, having information about the event and the people before you face them can be very comforting. The more you know about your listener, the less threatening they will seem.

Ask the following questions before speaking:

1. Why are these people here?
2. What have they been told about the topic?
3. What have they been told about the speaker?
4. How many people will be there?
5. What do they know about the topic?
6. What do they want to know about the topic?
7. How much time will I have?
8. How does my topic relate to this group?
9. Who are the key decision-makers in the group?
10. How will these people use this information?

Plus:

1. What questions am I likely to be asked?
2. Is a light-hearted or serious approach more appropriate for these people?

This basic information will serve you in two ways. First, you will be better able to prepare information, examples, and materials that relate directly to your listeners. This is always a benefit to speaker and listener. Second, fear of the unknown is normal—everyone experiences it. So, the more you know about your listeners, the less you will fear them.

Side 4: Know Your Channel

A channel is the medium used to convey your message. Your voice is a channel. Your speech is a channel. Your appearance is a channel. These all communicate messages to your listeners. Voice, speech, and appearance are not the only channels you will use, however. If you use a microphone, it becomes a channel. It helps you to carry your message as surely as your voice. Remember, the more you know about all aspects of speaking, the less fearsome the experience will be.

Let's take a closer look at a few of the more common channels that can affect you and your business speaking. Recognizing these channels will help you become a better business speaker.

The event may be an annual sales meeting, a regional conference, a departmental meeting, a motivational get-together. People's expectations vary at each event. This certainly will affect the way they receive your speech. If you know as much as possible about the event, you can anticipate listeners' expectations and tailor your speech accordingly.

If the situation is an annual conference where everyone is in an upbeat mood and having a good time, your speech should match that feeling. If you are asked to speak at a meeting concerned with union activities, your speech should be more serious and specific. The event at which you speak clearly affects listener expectations.

The *place* can have a big effect on the way your speech is received. There is a big difference between the way speeches are received when heard on Marco Island, Florida, and the way they are received when heard in the Gutman Library at Harvard University. As a speaker, you must take this into consideration.

You know from your own experience that listening to people speak at an assembly hall or classroom is different from listening to people speak at a picnic. Again, listeners are affected by the location. Recognize possible distractions, and perhaps make appropriate comments about the surroundings as you go through your speech. Marco Island, Florida, is a beautiful vacation resort on the Gulf of Mexico. Listeners are easily taken in by the beauty of the surroundings. Gutman Library at Harvard promotes a much more serious and formal state of mind. Listeners are more likely to give greater attention to you and your topic. Even though these are generalizations, be sure you evaluate the impact of the place on you and your listeners before speaking.

The *room* in which you deliver your speech can also affect both you and your listeners. Is it large or small, crowded or empty, warm or cold, bright or dim? Each of these and similar elements will have an effect on your speech. They are channels that affect your message.

Chapter Review

- Fear of speaking is normal. It is frequently named as the *most common* fear in business. Don't be concerned—it is a normal feeling of energy and anticipation.
- Both the psychological and the physiological aspects of this fear *can be controlled*.
- Each speaker can construct his or her own success strategy. Each will use a personalized system of control techniques.
- Understand the sides of the Silver Square:
  Know yourself.
  Know your topic.
  Know your listener.
  Know your channels.

- Use this knowledge to make yourself at ease and in control of effective business-speaking skills.

Practice Exercises

Action! Now that you understand the elements of the Silver Square, what do you do with this knowledge? Practice, practice, practice the following action exercises, which accompany each aspect of the Silver Square. The exercises should be done by you alone, at first. Then try them with a partner from your class.

Know Yourself

Exercise 1

On the left side of a blank sheet of paper, prepare a list of your most commonly repeated negative self-talk comments. On the right side of that paper, write a corresponding positive self-talk comment. Say these positive self-talk comments at least 10 times daily for at least three days before a speaking situation.

Exercise 2

Practice the diaphragmatic breathing exercise outlined earlier. Begin by watching your upper chest and diaphragm movements in a mirror as you practice. Do this exercise three times daily. Do it at midmorning, midafternoon, and between dinner and bedtime. Do it for 4 or 5 minutes each time, totaling 12 to 15 minutes daily.

Know Your Topic

Exercise 1

Once you have conducted a thorough assessment of your topic knowledge and have prepared your speech, here is a helpful exercise to practice your control over the fear of being caught off guard. It's called the Coffee Cup.

1. Write down on separate pieces of paper three of the most likely simple questions or comments you may receive after the speech.
2. Write down on separate pieces of paper three of the most likely difficult questions or comments you may receive after the speech.
3. Fold these six pieces of paper and place them in a coffee cup (or other similar container).
4. Deliver your speech out loud into a tape recorder.
5. Following the speech, choose one of the six folded slips of paper from the coffee cup. Read it aloud and answer the questions aloud.
6. Do this with each question.

7. Replay the tape and pay careful attention to those areas that sound weak, especially the question-and-answer period.
8. Restructure the weakest points.
9. Do it all again for confidence.
10. Do it all again for practice!

Exercise 2

Pretend that you are a listener who is directly opposed to the opinions and ideas that are to be presented in your speech. As that person, prepare an opposing three-minute speech. Include proofs that support your arguments. This exercise should help you understand the strong and weak points of your own topic.

Know Your Listener

Exercise 1

Plan a five-minute presentation to be given to your class. Use the listener analysis questions described in the chapter to focus your presentation. Share your answers with a coach or instructor. Ask your coach or classroom instructor how accurately you answered the listener analysis questions.

Exercise 2

Assume the role of a program chair who is making arrangements for a guest speaker. The guest speaker has asked you for as much background information as possible about the listeners so the speech can be most meaningful. What information about the listeners would you send to the guest speaker?

Know Your Channels

Exercise 1

Plan a five-minute speech to be given at your next class. As the speaker, what channels of communication would you need to control to ensure that your message is understood and accepted? Make a checklist of these channels and ask a classmate to review it for thoroughness.

Exercise 2

Attend a local meeting such as a town meeting, a school committee, a church group, or a political rally. Observe the channels of communication and evaluate how well speakers used, abused, or missed those channels.

Quick Quiz

1. What are at least five physical characteristics related to the fear of speaking?
2. Give at least three examples of dialogue illustrating attitudes of psychological reaction to the fear of speaking?
3. What is one of the negative results, in terms of speaking, that television promotes in children and adults?
4. What are the four sides of the Silver Square?
5. Is knowing your channel an important issue in overcoming speaking fear? Why?
6. How can knowing your own and your listeners' biases help you when you're planning your next speech?
7. What are three examples of positive self-talk?
8. What are the three types of breathing?
9. What is the appropriate breathing for speaking?
10. Why are the other types of breathing not helpful in controlling the psychological aspects of the fear of speaking?

3

Speaking Clearly

"When communicating in business, it is the ability to speak simply, clearly and concisely which will determine the acceptance of your ideas. Like making a first impression, you have only one opportunity to communicate and establish interest in your ideas."
William P. Bishop, CLU, *Vice President Western Division, State Mutual Companies*

Chapter Objectives

After reading this chapter, you will be able to:

1. Use vocal variety effectively.
2. Master techniques to improve your control of inflection, volume, duration, and intensity.
3. Define speech discrimination and guard against it.
4. Monitor your rate and pace of speaking.

This chapter provides both general guidelines for speaking clearly and specific techniques for improving your speaking quality. Most people realize that in a business environment, the first impression is based on appearance. Therefore, most of us try to control dress and grooming habits.

Our focus here is on another extremely important aspect of the first impression—the way you sound. Listeners are judging you, your talents, your intelligence, and much more by the way you sound. You have probably judged other people in the same manner. Speech discrimination is one of the oldest forms of discrimination on earth. We all do it. Therefore, it is vital to effective business speaking that you gain control over the way you sound, or risk reaching your full business potential.

In this chapter, we will discuss your voice and your speech quality. We will identify specific behaviors that may help or harm your ability to make a positive impression.

Voice-Speech Connection

The way you sound is a combination of how you use your voice and how you use your speech. Voice and speech are different. We will explore and identify the most important qualities to develop in these two areas.

Voice

Voice is the sound you are able to produce. Each person sounds different from others because of many factors. Some of these are:

- Size of your voice mechanism, including your larynx and vocal folds.
- General health.
- Environmental factors such as air quality.
- Diet, exercise, and whether or not you smoke.
- Stress and lifestyle.

One fear of business speakers is that they will sound monotonal, boring, and dull. Indeed, listeners are not favorably impressed with speakers who have these traits. To prevent this, be sure to have good *vocal variety;* that is, do different things with your voice to create interest and stress particular points.

The truth is that speakers who sound boring are probably not monotone—they are monopatterned. This means that they are using their voice and speech in a repeated and unchanging pattern. What puts people to sleep is the repetition of an unchanging sound. This is the same technique that is used to hypnotize people. The hypnotizer uses soft, mellow tones repeating and repeating the same words, sometimes swinging an object like a pocket watch or pendant back and forth in front of the hypnotizee. ''You are getting sleepy. You are getting sleepy, you are getting sleepy. You are getting sleepier, sleepier, sleepier, sleep, sleep, sleep." Good bye! Most people would fall asleep listening to something like that over and over and over. This is exactly what a speaker using a monopattern does.

There are several areas to concentrate on when developing effective vocal variety. Here are four: inflection, volume, duration, and intensity.

1. Inflection

Inflection is the stress or emphasis placed on a given word or sound to affect meaning. You can raise or lower inflection, like this:

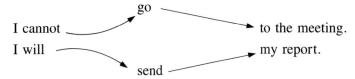

Inflection is particularly important at the end of a thought. A different meaning can be created by simply going up or down in inflection. For example, the following simple sentence can have three different meanings depending on how the end of the sentence is inflected.

Even inflection (factual):

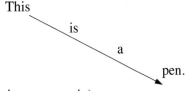

Down inflection (more emphatic):

Up inflection (questioning, uncertain):

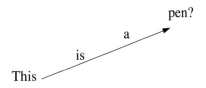

A common mistake in business speaking is the use of *up* inflection, sounding uncertain, when the speaker is not uncertain at all. Be sure to use *down* inflection when you want to sound authoritative.

2. Volume

Volume is very easy to manipulate. Simply increase the level of your volume, or decrease it. Both directions will create variety.

Say the following sentence so it can be heard five feet away:

I'm not responsible for this mess.

Now say the same sentence so it can be heard 50 feet away. Notice how the impact of the sentence changes for both speaker and listener.

3. Duration

Duration is the prolongation of individual sound. This can dramatically vary your sound and meaning, like this:

This is a ve-r-ry nice conference room.

Notice how much nicer the room seems. In fact, the more duration you use, the nicer the room will get. The opposite is also true—try it!

4. Intensity

Intensity is created by increasing the tension in the vocal mechanism. This is difficult to describe, but you can hear intensity when you hear someone speaking like Mickey Mouse or Goofy. Or think of the sound of the voice used by Marlon Brando for the character Don Corleone in *The Godfather*. *That* is the sound of intensity. Speakers often use intensity to emphasize the passion they feel for a particular topic, or to make a certain word or concept stand apart from the rest of a thought.

Speech

The other half of the voice-speech connection is speech. *Speech* is what you do with your voice—it is talking. This is a very simplistic and nonanatomical definition, but it serves our needs for business speaking. Simply put, speech is our main communication channel. We've just described ways to modulate your voice. Are there ways to control and use speech to create various effects? Well, we know what can happen if a person's speech is perceived as different from the norm. A speaker can be judged, and even be discriminated against, if his or her speech is found unacceptable in a given environment.

Speech discrimination is one of the oldest forms of discrimination in business. We all practice it. We discriminate for and against people because of the way they speak. It is so common that few of us even realize that we are discriminating.

Listeners make all kinds of decisions about you by the way you speak. This is especially true when they are hearing you for the first time. It may be at a staff meeting, greeting a new customer, gathering marketing information over the phone, or presenting data at a conference. Listeners decide your age, intelligence, qualifications, sense of humor, and more from the way you speak.

How often have you heard someone say, "I only spoke to Tom for a minute, but he sounds like a nice guy," or "Phyllis called and she certainly did sound upset." Of course, we judge these qualities in part by what was said; however, we also judge by the way they were said.

What are we listening to? What makes a difference to us? Naturally, ideas and information are important. Beyond that, we are listening to articulation, pronunciation, and speed.

Articulation

Articulation is the production of individual sounds. We manipulate and position six different articulators. They are:

1. Lips.
2. Teeth.
3. Tongue.
4. Velum (soft palate).
5. Pharyngeal wall.
6. Lower jaw.

The various combinations or placements produce the sounds in our language. For example, the word *desk* contains four sounds D-E-S-K. When these sounds are each articulated correctly, the word *desk* can be produced.

Pronunciation

Pronunciation is combining articulated sounds to make words that listeners understand. If the four sounds of the word *desk* are articulated correctly, but *combined* in a different order, such as D-E-K-S, an entirely different word is pronounced and understood by the listener. Speakers must master both articulation *and* pronunciation to be clearly understood.

Mumbling and sloppy speech do not make a positive impression in business speaking. Listeners are likely to equate sloppy speaking with sloppy work. No business wants that reputation. Therefore, it is important to have clear articulation and pronunciation. When speakers do not have control over articulation and pronunciation, they assimilate. *Assimilation* is the running together of words or sounds.

Assimilation is actually very common in American speech. Most people assimilate regularly. That doesn't make it effective and it is not our explanation or excuse for doing it! Assimilation is one of the most common weaknesses in business speaking. Remember, sloppy speech equals sloppy work. At least, that is what listeners may conclude.

Here are a few examples of common assimilations:

> Saying "wanna" instead of "want to."
> Saying "gimme" instead of "give me."
> Saying "gonna" instead of "going to."
> Saying "cancha" instead of "can't you."
> Saying "frinstance" instead of "for instance."

In business speaking, there are often times when we want to sound strong, decisive, or authoritative. In these cases, assimilation can be negative.

There is a way to control assimilation in business settings. We are not suggesting that you stop assimilating, only that you control it in those business-speaking situations when you want to sound authoritative and precise. You can control assimilation by careful use of *plosive* sounds. Plosive sounds are the eight sounds in the American English language that are produced by creating a small explosion of air. The plosive sounds are:

B	as in boy.
D	as in dog.
G	as in girl.
J	as in jump.
P	as in put.
T	as in toy.
K	as in kite.
CH	as in child.

You have two choices in producing these sounds. You can either explode them or implode them. You can say:

I'm moving to a new des. (implosion)

or:

I'm moving to a new des*k*. (explosion)

Another example:

This is a very special projec. (implosion)

or:

This is a very special projec*t*. (explosion)

Understanding the words *desk* or *project* is not the problem. Listeners are accustomed to filling in word endings that are frequently imploded. So what difference does it make? If listeners are accustomed to speakers dropping word endings, why be concerned?

There are two important business reasons to control assimilation through the use of plosive sounds:

1. *Clarity* produces efficiency. Being a clear speaker reduces the chance of error and misunderstanding. This is particularly true when your speech includes numbers or technical terms.
2. *Impression* is, as we already know, very important in business. Giving the impression of being in control, precise, accurate, and decisive is often critical.

Speed

Your rate of speaking affects both your voice and your speech. It is an important aspect of controlling mumbling, sloppy speech, and sounding boring. Controlling speed does not mean simply speaking faster or slower. Speed is divided into two components — rate and pace. There are no magic numbers that represent the best or proper speed. Each person, each situation, and each set of circumstances will dictate the most appropriate and effective speed for rate and pace.

Rate

Rate is the speed at which you put one word after the next. Rate of speaking in a normal conversation is approximately 130 to 150 words per minute. Rate of speed of speaking in a normal business presentation is approximately 150 to 175 words per minute. Business speakers can be faster because there is an understanding and agreement between the speaker and listener. The listener agrees to not speak during the presentation and to pay attention and follow the speaker's organization. The speaker agrees to be prepared, and allow appropriate time and place for questions. Of course, this is the ideal. Many business cultures encourage listeners to interrupt whenever they choose, and the speaker should be prepared to accommodate these interruptions.

Conversation is usually slower because there is less direction — both speaker and listener can change the topic, interrupt, or terminate the communication at any time. Naturally, it is possible to have animated conversation with a very fast rate of speaking.

Here is a paragraph containing 175 words. Practice reading it at different speeds to feel and hear the effect.

As the report progressed, it became clear that keeping on schedule would be directly related to the ability of the project manager to communicate with the client. Originally, it was thought that weekly meetings would suffice. It quickly became evident that daily communication would be necessary in the later stages of the work. However, travel and distance, unforeseen complications, cost, and even personality emerged as modifying variables. Personality and the individual differences in communication style became key stumbling blocks to the project's progress. The project manager preferred to make a quick phone call and relate the overall progress for the day. The client preferred a more detailed report of specific aspects of the daily tasks. These differences in communication style caused irritations and misunderstandings. These often led to indecision and delay, which created havoc with the schedule and increased the budget. Eventually, it was decided that both the project manager and the client would allow their ''next-in-charge'' to handle the daily discussions. They got along fine and the project was finished within the budget.

Pace

Pace is the distance you put between the thoughts you present when speaking. It is impossible to indicate a number of thoughts per minute. This will vary greatly. Information and ideas that are new to the listener, complicated, or technical usually require more pace time between them. Topics that are familiar to the listener or easy to understand usually require less pace time. Controlling the pace of speaking is comparable to the timing of credits that roll by at the end of a movie. All the information—the titles, the names, and so on—is there, but depending on how fast they roll by on the screen, you may or may not be able to read and understand them all. It's the same with speaking and listening. Your listener may wish you would slow down or speed up flow of information and ideas. Controlling this speed is controlling pace in speaking.

In writing, we control this speed and organization for the reader by separating our information and ideas into paragraphs. When readers see one paragraph end and another begin, they know there will be a new thought presented. They can choose to read the next paragraph or go back and review the last one until they are comfortable enough to move on. Listeners do not have that luxury—they are at the mercy of the speaker. Listeners cannot go back and review the last point the speaker made. They are compelled to "listen on" to the next point. Therefore, speakers must be sensitive to listeners and control the pace of speaking.

The following paragraphs are about a report on smoking in a building. Try reading them aloud in one minute. Change the pace time by allowing more silence between the paragraphs. Notice how your mind uses the time you provide between thoughts. First allow one second, then two seconds, then three seconds.

The brief report provides the results and recommendations that are the outcome of the unified task force on smoking in the building.

Each of you reading this report is expected to evaluate the facts and circumstances surrounding this issue and vote on the recommended actions outlined in this report.

The task force surveyed 137 employees. These employees were chosen at random from each of the four divisions of the company. Each division provided approximately 35 employee interviewees. The five members of the task force conducted the face-to-face interviews over a period of four weeks. A copy of the questions asked is included in the appendix of the report. Recommendations based on the analysis of this interview information can also be found in the appendix.

Because each of you is required to vote on the implementation of the unified task force recommendations, it is suggested that you review these recommendations carefully before attending the staff meeting to be held on the 30th of this month.

The most important point regarding speaking speed is that you can and should control it. After careful analysis of each speaking opportunity, be sure to plan the appropriate rate and pace. Practice your speech out loud, tape it, play it back, and listen to the effect.

Chapter Review

- Speaking clearly means having control over your voice and speech. Vocal variety will prevent you from creating boring and monotone patterns of repeated sounds. To avoid these negative patterns, concentrate on varying your:

    Inflection.

    Volume.

    Duration.

    Intensity.

- To control speech, concentrate on articulation, pronunciation, and assimilation.

- Speaking clearly also entails regulating speaking speed by monitoring rate and pace. Rate and pace will vary according to such variables as:

    Speaker familiarity with the topic.

    Audience familiarity with the topic.

    Speaker clarity.

    Use of visuals.

    Time and setting.

- Remember that failing to master clear speaking may result in speech discrimination at work, a common but avoidable result of less-than-careful speech habits.

Practice Exercises

Exercise 1

To gain control over your articulation and pronunciation, try these exercises every day.

1. Open your mouth wide and close it. Do not be afraid to open your mouth W I D E. This is a stretching exercise. Practice this five times.
2. Round your lips and protrude them as far as you can. Say ''OO'' and repeat five times.

3. Spread your lips back in a *big* smile. Feel the muscles pulling around your chin and neck area. Repeat five times.

4. Thrust your upper lip forward. Thrust your lower lip forward. Repeat five times.

5. Stretch your upper lip down. Stretch your bottom lip up. Repeat five times.

6. Raise the right side of your mouth. Raise the left side of your mouth. Be sure your whole face is involved in this movement. The muscles of your face must move freely to show expression. Repeat five times.

7. Protrude your tongue without touching your top or bottom lip. This will be helpful for good production of sounds such as *th*. Repeat 10 times.

8. Point the tip of your tongue up and touch your top lip; then the right corner of your mouth; then the left; then point it down toward your chin. Repeat 10 times.

9. Rotate your tongue around the inside of your mouth over your upper teeth, then your bottom teeth. Repeat 10 times.

10. Raise the tip of your tongue and touch the roof of your mouth, then slowly bring it back toward your soft palate. Repeat 10 times.

11. Let the tip of your tongue touch the roof of your mouth. Flap it up and down, making sure you produce strong lah, lah, lah, nah, nah, nah sounds. Repeat 10 times.

12. Practice articulating A-E-I-O-U, opening your mouth as widely as you can, using the articulators to the point you feel a tingling sensation. Repeat 10 times.

Exercise 2

This exercise will help control assimilation or sloppy speech by strengthening your use of plosive sounds. Read these sentences into a tape recorder. Be sure to explode each of the plosive sounds. It will sound strange, but that's expected. Explode every plosive sound you see. Then replay the tape and listen for the plosive sounds. If you miss a sound, or it was not clear, reread these sentences until you get the sounds right. Remember, it's OK for these sentences to sound strange!

1. Mister Bishop greeted the new client.
2. Our fax machine isn't working properly.
3. The market for computers will get bigger next year.
4. Work-related issues dominated the trip.
5. The new plant is not easy to get to.
6. Parking is a problem for most overnight workers.

7. Office desks don't get cleaned.
8. The time card machine is being replaced.
9. Most overtime work is compensated.
10. It's easy to get in at eight, but hard to get started.

Quick Quiz

1. What are the two characteristics of clear speaking you must develop to become a successful speaker?
2. What skill must be developed to prevent sounding boring and dull?
3. What is assimilation?
4. What is a plosive sound?
5. What are the eight plosive sounds?
6. What is the speed in speaking in business presentations?
7. What is the difference between rate and pace?
8. What are the four key aspects of vocal quality?
9. What is the most important point regarding speaking speed?
10. What tool is most helpful to listen to and use in practicing your speech and exercising your voice?

Prepare and Organize for Business Speaking

"Communicating, whether to financial analysts or managers, is essential to business success. When speaking to a group: (1) know your audience—gear your comments to their interest and sophistication; (2) keep it simple—be organized and use direct language; (3) be yourself—that's who they came to hear!"
Ben Cammarata, *President and Chief Executive Officer, TJX Companies, Inc.*

Chapter Objectives

After reading this chapter, you will be able to:

1. Understand and use inductive reasoning patterns in your speeches.
2. Undertand and use deductive reasoning patterns in your speeches.
3. Use the four-step outline approach to organizing your speeches.
4. Use the numerical transition technique of organization in your speeches.

This chapter covers effective organizational skills for business speaking. We focus on two skills that are valuable at every level in business and in any speaking situation. These two skills are flexible, practical, and, above all, useful.

The first skill is the ability to organize material in the specific *patterns of reasoning* we all use to understand and process information.

The second organizational skill is the ability to use a specific outlining format for delivering ideas in a clear, succinct manner. It is called, simply, *the four-step outline*.

Patterns of Reasoning

The ability to understand how other people organize their thoughts—the patterns they prefer in their reasoning—is valuable at every level in business and in every business-speaking situation. If you can understand your listeners' pattern of reasoning, you can be more effective in responding to and interacting with them.

You should first also identify your own pattern of reasoning. How do you like to organize your ideas when you speak with others? Each of us has a particular pattern that we prefer and use most of the time. If that pattern happens to match the pattern being used by the person with whom you are speaking, things go along smoothly. Matching your pattern of business speaking to your listeners' patterns can go a long way toward success in business.

People usually arrange their thoughts in one of two patterns: inductive or deductive.

Inductive pattern

In *inductive* organization, people present specific arguments, facts, figures, examples, or other bits of evidence on their way to a general conclusion. Graphically, the inductive pattern looks like this:

x_1
x_2 Specific information
x_3 leading to a
x_4

$\{X\}$ General conclusion

Here's an example:

> "The office supplies are very difficult to get to. Most people who use them work on the second floor and the supply closet is on the third floor. I'm going to relocate the supply closet from the third floor to the second floor."

Specific reason 1	Supplies difficult to get to.
Specific reason 2	Most people work on 2nd floor.
Specific reason 3	Supplies currently on 3rd floor.
General conclusion	I'll move the supply closet.

This speaker gave three specific reasons (any number will do) why he reached the general conclusion to move the office supplies to the second floor. This is a specific to general organization of ideas.

> "Margaret, your work over the last six months has been outstanding. You did an excellent job on preparing the Acme proposal. You seem to have a good grasp on how to handle the flurry of customer requests we've been receiving lately. And you're especially good with people over the phone. Therefore, I'm recommending you for a raise."

In outline form, the argument is

Specific reason 1	Six months' outstanding work.
Specific reason 2	Excellent on Acme proposal.
Specific reason 3	Good with customer requests.
Specific reason 4	Good phone skills.
General conclusion	Recommend raise.

Here, the speaker gave four specific reasons for the general conclusion to recommend Margaret for a raise.

Deductive pattern

In the *deductive* pattern, people present their general conclusion first, then back it up with specific reasons. Graphically, the deductive pattern looks like this:

$\{X\}$ General conclusion

x_1
x_2 Supported by
x_3 specific reasons
x_4

Here's an example of this pattern:

> "We should buy our copy machine supplies from INTECH. They deliver for free, they have an 800 phone number, plus they give discounts on every order over $100.00."

We can outline this argument as follows:

General conclusion   Buy from INTECH.
Specific reason 1   Free delivery.
Specific reason 2   800 phone number.
Specific reason 3   Discounts.

This speaker made an immediate statement of opinion—"We should buy our copy machine supplies from INTECH." The speaker then followed with three specific reasons why she believes that. This is general to specific organization of ideas.

Another example should help to clarify the point.

> "The presentation will make all the difference in whether we get the NUFOLD client contract. We have all the right qualifications and they want people who communicate well. Because their image is so public, they'll want to work with people who give a positive public image and can think on their feet."

In outline form:

General conclusion	Good presentation will win NUFOLD contract.
Specific reason 1	Good qualifications already.
Specific reason 2	Good communication skills.
Specific reason 3	Positive public image.
Specific reason 4	Think on your feet.

In this example of deductive organization, the speaker made it clear immediately that she believed the presentation was the most important factor in getting the NUFOLD contract. Then, the speaker proceeded to elaborate on the reasons for this belief.

It is important to note that both inductive and deductive patterns of reasoning can be correct and effective, depending on the circumstances. The more you understand the differences between these patterns, the more effective you will be as a speaker. People like to do business with people with whom they can easily communicate and interact. So if you can determine that a co-worker or a customer is a deductive type of thinker-communicator, you can adapt your own speaking organization to match his or hers and help ensure a comfortable interaction.

The question of which pattern to use is difficult to answer. There are no absolute rules. However, there are some indicators that may help you decide. Here are a few suggestions about which pattern to use when:

Inductive	*Deductive*
• With technical topics.	• With emotional topics.
• With unfamiliar audiences.	• With audiences that you know.
• When building a personal case.	• When the time limit is tight.

Four-Step Outline

The second skill that is valuable at every level in business and in any speaking situation is knowing how to create a four-step outline. This is a simple, direct, logical method for organizing your thoughts. It helps a speaker prepare and present a speech. It helps a listener follow and file the information and ideas presented. The four-step outline consists of (1) introduction, (2) benefits, (3) body, and (4) conclusion.

Step 1: Introduction

Tell the listeners what you *are* going to tell them and, if appropriate, what you *are not* going to tell them. Tell them approximately how long you will be speaking and whether you will have handout materials. Tell them if and when you would welcome questions. Tell them if it's important to take notes. Tell them any special instructions or requests you may have and anything else you believe they should know about what and how you're going to be speaking. It may not always be appropriate to give all of this information. Some listeners know very well what the limits and expectations are; for them, it would sound unnecessary to go into such simple detail. So think carefully about your listeners' levels of knowledge, their relationship with you, their familiarity with each other, and the setting before deciding how much detail is needed for step 1.

The intent of step 1 is to give your listeners a clear understanding of *what* is about to happen. A very effective method for doing this is the *numerical transition technique*. Assign a number to each of the main points you will cover in your speech. Then, simply list those main points by number to your listeners. For example, "Today I will speak about three issues—number one, scheduling; number two, personnel; and number three, funding." The introduction not only gives your listeners a comfortable feeling about the topic, but it also helps them feel comfortable about your confidence and competence.

Normally, this step is short and direct. It should be completed in less than one minute.

Step 2: Benefits

Tell the listeners *why* they should listen to you talk about this topic. Whether or not they ultimately agree with you, how *do* you expect them to benefit by listening? Some benefits that you might mention in step 2 as reasons why they should listen to you include:

- Making their jobs easier.
- Improving their health.
- Relieving stress.
- Stimulating creativity.
- Providing security.
- Increasing their income.

As a speaker, you should be able to tell at least one, and maybe more, good reasons why they should listen to you. The intent is to give your listeners a clear understanding of why your ideas are valuable. Many speakers find this the most difficult of all the steps in the four-step outline. Business speakers frequently say things like, "They know why this is important," or "They invited me to speak, I'm sure they know the value of what I'm saying.'' This is a big mistake. There will be times when listeners have no clear idea how your thoughts apply to them. Perhaps their boss told them to attend. Maybe they came with friends. Maybe they came to make friends by networking. In any case, you cannot hurt your cause by giving a short, direct answer to their question, ''What's in it for me?'' After all, if you can't think of a reason for them to listen, they probably can't either. If you can't identify the reasons why people should listen to you speak on a certain topic, then why are you speaking to them at all?

This step is also short and should be delivered in less than one minute.

Step 3: Body

The body will be the longest portion of the speech. Here you will present your ideas supported by facts, examples, demonstrations, and so on. The body is where you lay out any directives or details and where you develop your ideas and explain them.

The numerical transition technique, discussed in step 1, is appropriate in this step as well. Use the same numbering system you used in step 1 to help you and your listeners move from one point to the next. In your introduction, you might have said, ''The three areas I'll be speaking about today are (1) scheduling, (2) personnel, and (3) funding.'' When you reach step 3, the body of your presentation, you will have a built-in organizational pattern. After you finish filling in the details under your first point, simply use the numerical transition technique to move to your second point. For example, ''Next, I'll move on to point 2, personnel.''

The numerical transition technique is a simple, direct, and easy-to-follow method for helping both speaker and listener organize information. Be certain that you say and do what you promised in step 1 of the outline. The time required to complete Step 3 will vary according to your need, your listeners' needs, the topic, and the setting.

Step 4: Conclusion

Recap the main points of your speech. This step has two parts.

Review The Most Important Points.   Don't go back and review everything you said — review only the most important points. This means that you must know what the most important points are. Of course, you should know these even before your presentation begins. Review the highlights of these points and state exactly, in brief sentences, what you want your listeners to remember.

Make An Action Statement.   Now that you have presented your ideas clearly, tell the listeners what they could do with that information. This is an opportunity for you to demonstrate your understanding of the topic by suggesting appropriate implementation. Not all presentations will require an action statement, so analyze your situation carefully before taking this step. But if it is warranted, don't hesitate to make an action statement such as:

> "Please include this information in your scheduling meetings. Feel free to come to my office for further assistance."

The time required to deliver step 4 will vary according to what topics have been covered in the preceding steps of the outline. Normally, step 4 should take no longer than four minutes.

The accompanying worksheet is based on the four-step outline. Write your notes regarding each step in the Notes column under the appropriate step number on the worksheet. In the column labeled Reminders, you can write notes regarding the use of audiovisual aids, emphasizing specific words, opportunities for listener participation, or particular areas to change your speed of speaking. The worksheet can help organize your ideas. Learn to use it each time you prepare a speech.

Four-Step Outline Worksheet

Topic:

Notes	*Reminders*
Step 1: Introduction	
Step 2: Benefits	
Step 3: Body	
Step 4: Conclusion	

Here's an example of a completed four-step outline of a business speech.

Four-Step Outline Worksheet Topic: Day Care Center	
Notes	*Reminders*
Step 1: Introduction • Introduce topic and time needed (one minute). • Define changing work force. • Both parents working.	• working mothers • older people • latch-key children
Step 2: Benefits • How to ensure less stress for employees. • How to ensure less absenteeism for Company.	• more productivity • use visuals
Step 3: Body • Absenteeism cost up. • Day care a necessity. • Recommend company site and costs.	• facts & figures • set aside second floor?
Step 4: Conclusion • Both parents must work. • Reduce employee stress. • Increase employee effectiveness. • Sign petition to recommend on-site day-care center.	• use visuals • smile and gesture

Here's another example that might be used for a business speech.

Four-Step Outline Worksheet Topic: Good Speech Is Good Business	
Notes	*Reminders*
Step 1: Introduction • Introduce topic and time needed. • Define good speech and good business.	• tell story about CEO • smile *continued*

<table>
<tr><td colspan="2" align="center">Four-Step Outline Worksheet

Topic: Good Speech Is Good Business</td></tr>
<tr><td>Notes</td><td>Reminders</td></tr>
</table>

Notes	Reminders
Step 2: Benefits • Employees and customers benefit. • Presents confident and competent impression. • Helps make work go smoothly.	• ask participation • morale • learning environment • communication
Step 3: Body • Describe four-step outline for better speaking. • Usable in formal and informal speaking. • Use employee training as example.	• visual aids • parties • meetings • get memo from meeting
Step 4: Conclusion • Good speech is good business. • Smoother communication. • Improve impression. • Use four-step outline.	• to organize next meeting • be upbeat

Chapter Review

- Good organizational skills are extremely valuable in business.
- As you develop the specific technical talents required to do a good job, remember to exercise your own organizational skills.
- The two basic, broad organizational patterns that people use are inductive and deductive.
- Using the four-step outline helps you organize your speech and helps your listeners follow your thinking. The four steps to master are:

  1. Introducing your topic.
  2. Stating the benefits.
  3. Presenting the body.
  4. Stating your conclusion.

- Combining your understanding of speech patterns with mastery of the four-step outline will make you polished and persuasive!

Practice Exercises

These exercises should be done with another student, an instructor, a friend, or anyone who can be a critical and informed listener. You may wish to have two or three classmates in your study group give you feedback on the techniques you are practicing. If you cannot coordinate a group, use a tape recorder and assess your own progress. Tape yourself going through the exercise, then play it back. Be your own honest critic.

Exercise 1

Make an inductive speech on the following three topics:

1. Violence on television.
2. Capital punishment.
3. Gun control laws.

Exercise 2

Make a deductive speech on the same three topics.

Exercise 3

Ask an inductive question on the following three topics:

1. Drinking age.
2. Dress codes in companies.
3. 55 MPH speed limit.

Exercise 4

Ask a deductive question on the same three topics.

Exercise 5

Use the four-step outline worksheet shown in the chapter to prepare an outline for a one-minute presentation on each of the following three topics:

1. Homelessness in the United States.
2. Best age for marriage.
3. Athletes' pay scale.

Now, deliver each of these presentations to a class partner. Do not exceed one minute for each. Repeat this exercise using a 30-second time limit.

Quick Quiz

1. What are the main patterns of reasoning?
2. What is another name for the general to specific pattern?
3. What is another name for the specific to general pattern?
4. What are the four steps in the four-step outline?
5. In step 1 of the four-step outline, what is an effective method for giving listeners a clear understanding of what topics or points you will be making?
6. What purpose does step 2 serve?
7. In what step of the four-step outline do you develop your ideas?
8. What must you do in step 4 to get a response from your listeners?
9. Which step should be the longest portion of your presentation?
10. Which step do many speakers find most difficult to do and therefore may eliminate altogether?

Informing and Persuading

"Industrial leadership in the 90s requires the application of a full range of speech communication skills in order to satisfy diverse stakeholders ranging from customers, employees, shareholders, and neighbors to special interest groups. It has never been more important to really know your audience."
Bill Schwalm, *Senior Manager, Programs-Manufacturing, Polaroid*

Chapter Objectives

After reading this chapter, you will be able to:

1. Use effective listener analysis techniques.
2. Differentiate between informative and persuasive speaking techniques.
3. Use pathos, ethos, and logos in persuasive speaking.
4. Understand and recognize mixed messages.

This chapter will help you understand the difference between informative and persuasive business speaking. We'll introduce three effective methods for delivering information. We'll present a listener analysis technique that applies to almost every speaking situation. Finally, we'll explain the only three ways to persuade listeners on any topic and show you how to incorporate them into your business speaking.

Business Speaking Mix

Business speaking requires a mixture of information and persuasion. They are both critical, and you will use both in different situations and for different reasons. The distinction between these two types of speaking is that *informative speaking* lists data and impartially clarifies and enlightens with no particular goal other than making information clear. *Persuasive speaking* urges a partisan decision, favors a position, and tries to gain acceptance. Informative business speaking will be found in many settings, including:

- Committee reports.
- Briefings.
- Progress reports.
- Conferences.
- Staff/department meetings.
- Teaching and training.

An informative speaker's intent is to *report*.

Persuasive speaking will also be found in many settings, including:

- Meetings.
- Sales situations.
- Client presentations.
- Negotiations.
- Budget hearings.

A persuasive speaker's intent is to *influence*.

There may be many more settings for both informative and persuasive speaking, and you will find that these types of speaking may overlap. What is supposed to be informative is persuasive, and vice versa. This can happen by accident, oversight, misunderstanding, or calculated planning. You will also find instances where information itself will be persuasive. As an effective business speaker, you must understand the reasons for using informative and persuasive speaking and be in control of when and how you use these methods. Such control not only increases your self-confidence, it also helps impress others. They will recognize your organizational skills and mastery of effective speaking skills. This is often seen as a sign of your business capabilities.

Whether your business speaking will be persuasive or informative, you will need to analyze your listeners. You must know as much as possible about them to make wise decisions about the preparation and presentation of your ideas. The Presentation Preparation Information (PPI) questionnaire will help you with listener analysis.

Presentation Preparation Information

The PPI form consists of 10 questions to ask prior to the business-presentation process. These 10 questions relate to listener analysis, and therefore your needs:

1. Why am I speaking to these listeners?
2. Why are they listening?
3. What relationship do we have?
4. What relationship do listeners have to each other?
5. What do they know about this topic?
6. What would they like to know?
7. How will they use this information?
8. What are they doing the day before I speak?
9. What will they be doing the day after?
10. What are the logistics of the event: time, location, room description, temperature, seating, lighting, and sound?

The information you gather from these 10 questions will make the job of preparing a speech much easier. In addition, your listeners will be more likely to respond positively if they feel that your research has helped you prepare specifically for them.

Being Informative

When your business speaking requires that you be informative, you must understand precisely what that means. There are at least three major opportunities for being informative in business speaking:

1. *Telling* involves the direct transfer of information from speaker to listener. The speaker has no other purpose than to transmit data with no specific concern for what is done with the data.
2. *Teaching* involves telling and the use of techniques designed to help listeners understand and learn the information being transferred. In addition, the speaker tests or quizzes the listeners to ensure understanding.

3. *Training* involves telling and teaching. In addition, the speaker requires the listeners to demonstrate understanding of the information through performance, display, or utilization of the data.

There are many applications for each of these kinds of informative speaking. In fact, it is common to find them intertwined during business speaking. As speaker and listener, you must be aware of the differences.

Whichever you choose — telling, teaching, or training — here are three important guidelines for effective, informative business speaking, the *three Cs:*

1. *Be clear* in your thinking, your organizing, and especially your language. Identify your themes (what you want your listeners to remember above all else) and supporting ideas; state them clearly.
2. *Be concise* in your expressions of thought. Use single, declarative sentences.
3. *Be consistent* in your use of language. Listeners shouldn't be tricked or have to work hard to follow your ideas. Use the same vocabulary when you speak.

We will discuss these three Cs in more detail in Chapter 7. At this point it may help to remember the K.I.S.S. method: Keep It Short & Simple.

Being Persuasive

When your business speaking requires that you be a persuasive speaker, draw on the information below. Persuasive speaking will be valuable in a wide variety of settings, from selling products to convincing the boss to give you a raise.

The three modes of persuasion we discuss were originally introduced by Aristotle in *The Rhetoric*. Through the centuries, these three modes have endured. While people have changed, the names, purpose, definitions, and values of these three techniques have not changed — they are as powerful today as they ever were.

Ethos.   *Ethos* means ethics. Ethos is the speaker's ability to persuade listeners because they know the speaker is an ethical, credible expert on the subject. If you have ethos, you are credible. We see examples of ethos in TV commercials that use a famous movie star, a doctor, or other recognized authority to promote products. These promoters may or may not be true experts, but if listeners believe in them, that's ethos at work.

Pathos.   *Pathos* means emotion. Pathos is the ability to persuade listeners by touching an emotional cord. Pathos is very powerful, easy to use, and very effective. TV commercials are dominated by pathos. We see it in the use of cute kids, singles, sexy people, beautiful scenery, and families on front porches. (Didn't we describe just about every TV commercial on the air?)

Logos. *Logos* means logic. Logos is the use of facts, figures, statistics, black-and-white data, and research studies to back up an assertion or make a point. Very few TV commercials use logos. When you do find logos, it is often confused by either ethos or pathos. Cold relief commercials documenting the speed of relief with facts and graphs often include a medical professional (ethos) or a sickly but cute child (pathos). Logos may not be popular in TV commercials, but it is very popular in business speaking. In fact, it is often overused to the point of ineffectiveness.

Putting Your Skills to Work

Being persuasive and understanding that ethos, pathos, and logos are effective mean that you must answer two questions. The first is, "How can I build ethos, pathos, and logos right into my speaking?" The answer to this question will vary greatly, depending on many factors, including:

- Time of day.
- Your mood.
- Size of group.
- Your speaking skills.
- Purpose of speaking.
- Location and setting.
- Available support materials.
- Past experience.
- Knowledge of subject.
- Weather.
- Seating arrangement.
- Your appearance.
- Your voice.
- Choice of words.
- Facial expression.
- Listener information.

It is not necessary to build all three modes of persuasion into your speaking events. The dynamic nature of communication and the various needs of listeners will compel you to evaluate every application of ethos, pathos, and logos separately. Each of the factors in the preceding list influences the combination of ethos, pathos, and logos in your speaking.

The second question you must answer to use these modes of persuasion in your business speaking is, "How do I deal with the fact that they are already in my speaking?" That's right. You use ethos, pathos, and logos every time you speak. You may not intend to do so; you may not even be thinking about it. And your listeners may not be listening or looking for them either, especially by their names—but they are there. Many of us are keenly aware of how we look and what signals, messages, or impressions are created by the style, size, color, and combination of our clothes. In fact, clothing is one of the most obvious expressions of how you already communicate ethos, pathos, and logos.

What about your speech? How does your clarity, organization, speed, or vocabulary affect your listeners? Most people are careful not to use certain kinds of language in certain kinds of places or around certain people. For instance, you wouldn't use racist or sexist language at any meeting, even if you hear this type of language being used by others. You would never swear at a meeting, no matter how comfortable you felt with the participants.

There may be some cases where it seems as if this language would be accepted. However, make and keep to your own rule: NEVER use language that could be considered offensive. It makes good business sense to err on the side of politeness and decorum. You don't want to run the risk of being labeled as a potentially embarassing representative of your organization.

This same self-control, which we exercise in good taste, can be brought to controlling ethos, pathos, and logos in business speaking. Accents, for example, can have a pathos effect on listeners. Northerners might judge speakers with a southern accent as being "slow-witted and backward." Southerners who hear a New York accent might judge speakers as "fast talkers" trying to put something over on them. These are pathos reactions. Speech discrimination is alive and well. So, because of negative pathos due to an accent, speakers may lose ethos because their listeners won't accept the speaker's logos. Did you follow that? Read it again, and think about it.

Likewise, have you ever known someone who tries to create a credible impression (ethos) by using big words? Or perhaps you got home very late one night only to find your parents waiting up for you. You tried your ethos ("Take my word for it, traffic was awful"); that didn't work. You tried logos ("There's a logical explanation for this, Dad . . ."); that didn't work. So, finally, you tried your pathos ("Oh, Mom, I'm so sorry; I'll never do this again."); sometimes, that worked.

Refining Your Skills

For many speakers, it takes trial and error over the years to refine the persuasive skills they possess today. You may not have called them ethos, pathos, and logos, but you certainly have been using them yourself. Today, you use them without even thinking about them. They have worked so well for you over the years that they have become second nature to you. However, your business-speaking effectiveness will increase as you refine your skills of analysis, control, and practice, and develop your own methods of using ethos, pathos, and logos.

Here are a few examples of expressions you will often hear, or words very similar to them. They are used by business speakers in all walks of life:

Ethos	*Pathos*	*Logos*
"As project director for . . ."	"We have a sincere desire to keep our customer relations very healthy."	"The committee report indicates a 6.5 percent differential."
"Our vice president has authorized me to . . ."	"This is a terrific example of sloppy recordkeeping."	"Market demographics point to a changing customer base in the Southeast region."
"During the six years I have been working on this project. . ."	"Thank you for the enjoyable and enlightening get-together."	"A positive response to the proposal will result from the accurate interpretation of research data."

Beware!

There is one caution we must put forth: Don't send mixed messages. This mistake is made easily and frequently.

Mixed messages occur when a speaker says or does something that he or she believes gives a certain message, but that is received very differently by the listener. For example, let's take the logos statement: "Twenty-three percent of the new sales will be generated in the Northeast." If this logos statement is delivered with a pathos smile, it may well be interpreted differently than if it were presented with a frown. Listeners can easily be confused and not know whether to accept the logos in the content or the pathos in the delivery. These mixed messages can occur in any combination among ethos, pathos, and logos. They are the result of speakers not matching the message and the means of delivering the message. Can you imagine a judge appearing in court to try a serious case wearing a clown suit? Most young people have experienced the lecture on using drugs delivered by adults who smoke and drink. These are mixed messages.

In business speaking, sending mixed messages is a *very* common problem. Some examples:

- Speakers who *say* they "really want your business" while looking out the window instead of at the client.

- Speakers who sound dull and monotone while telling the customer how "very pleased we are to serve you."

- Speakers who *believe* they are the best qualified to perform a task but who say, "I *think* I will provide the best service available."

These are mixed messages. Listeners get confused. They don't know what to believe. Who suffers? The speaker does. Be careful to match your content and delivery.

This is why corporations rely on speech coaches, public relations firms, and media experts to choose just the right location, time of day, type of room, color of clothes, and so on, to make major announcements or hold press conferences. We see glaring examples of efforts to control mixed messages during campaign time. Politicians are careful to choose the right city or farm background, factory workers or office workers, children or senior citizens to create just the right impression. They want no mixed messages.

This is not to say that you can't mix ethos, pathos, and logos. Certainly you can and perhaps should mix them. The point is to be careful that mixed messages don't occur accidently.

Ethos, pathos, and logos are the only three ways to persuade listeners. *Persuade* is the key word. We are not talking about *coerce*. We recognize that coercion, the threat of physical harm, does work. But the focus in business speaking in on persuasion, and that means mastering ethos, pathos, and logos.

Chapter Review

- Business speaking is a combination of information and persuasion.
- Both informative and persuasive speaking require effective listener analysis.
- Use the 10 PPI questions to understand the listeners.
- Informative speaking includes telling, teaching, and training approaches.
- Telling is the simple transmission of data.
- Teaching is transmitting data, then testing for understanding.
- Training is telling, teaching, then requiring a demonstration of the learned information.
- Informative business speaking should be clear, concise, and consistent.
- Persuasive speaking utilizes ethos, pathos, and logos.
- Ethos is the use of credibility, reputation, and ethics.
- Pathos is the use of emotion.
- Logos is the use of logic.
- Be careful not to accidentally send mixed messages unknowingly by mixing ethos, pathos, and logos.

Practice Exercises

1. Prepare and deliver a two-minute speech persuading listeners to grant you a pay raise. Use only logos.
2. Prepare and deliver a two-minute speech informing listeners of the happenings at a recent school event.
3. Listen to, analyze, and identify the modes of persuasion in a political speech.
4. Listen to, analyze, and identify the modes of persuasion in a TV commercial.
5. Identify separate examples of telling, teaching, and training found in your school experience.
6. Identify two examples of mixed messages in a business or political speech.
7. Prepare and present a five-minute persuasive speech using at least three visuals and utilizing ethos, pathos, and logos at various times in the speech. Accompany this speech with an outline that has ethos, pathos, and logos. On the outline, identify when, where, and how you will use these modes of persuasion.

Quick Quiz

1. What is the purpose of informative speaking?
2. What is the purpose of persuasive speaking?
3. When is it necessary to use the PPI questionnaire?
4. What are the three major opportunities for being informative?
5. What are the three guidelines (three Cs) for effective, informative business speaking?
6. What are the three modes of persuasion?
7. What are at least 10 factors that will affect ethos, pathos, and logos?
8. What is one of the most obvious expressions of how you already communicate ethos, pathos, and logos?
9. What is a mixed message?
10. What two factors must match in order to avoid mixed messages?

6 Participating in Meetings

"Developing good communication skills is not a passive process, but one whose practice and experience reinforce them until they become habits . . . habits that are transferrable outside the business environment."
Diana Thomas, *Director of Marketing, Critical Care America*

Chapter Objectives

After reading this chapter, you will be able to:

1. Recognize and define the main types of business meetings.
2. Define and understand hidden agendas.
3. Understand the purpose and format of information meetings and problem-solving meetings.
4. Use a six-step problem-solving technique.

Meetings, meetings, meetings. You're going to attend a lot of meetings in business. You'll even attend meetings to plan meetings. You'll meet people whose business is solely to plan meetings — they don't go to meetings, they just plan them. In this chapter, we review the most common types of meetings, including perhaps your most important meeting — the job interview. We'll discuss the type of speaking that is usually part of these meetings, the different types of people who attend all these meetings, and the skills necessary to lead meetings. Finally, because so many meetings are focused on problems, we will teach you a six-step problem-solving technique.

What Is a Meeting?

There is a common misconception about meetings. Many people believe that a business meeting involves a group of people discussing problems. Yes, that certainly describes a meeting; but in business, this definition is entirely too narrow. A meeting is any time two or more people exchange ideas. It can occur any time, any place, for any reason. Business meetings happen all the time, so you must be prepared all the time.

Meetings are not like presentations. Presentations are special events that can be planned, timed, controlled, directed, and practiced. Meetings are seldom that rigidly defined. Meetings can be impromptu, free-wheeling, disjointed, and disguised. Yes, disguised. Unlike a business presentation, which is usually identified as an important significant event, a business meeting is often not even labeled as a meeting. You may not even know a meeting happened until days later when someone says, ''I heard about your meeting.'' ''What meeting? We were walking to lunch and talking. That's not a meeting.'' *Wrong.* Don't be fooled, be ready.

There are three main categories of business meetings:

1. *Formal* meetings are those that are business meetings scheduled in advance. Participants are invited in advance; an agenda, or plan, is prepared; a time limit is set; a format for the conduct of the meeting is followed; and a leader is selected. In addition, participants are often asked to prepare and present or discuss their thoughts on the topic of the meeting. Finally, there are objectives or a goal to be achieved through the meeting.

2. *Informal* business meetings have much less structure, although they may have some of the same elements as formal meetings. For instance, informal meetings may have a leader or an agenda. However, they are normally more laid-back. They frequently have no time limit, participants are not asked for prepared presentations, and often the specific objectives and goals are not as clearly identified. *Social meetings* are a type of informal meeting. They may be conducted at work, with people from work, but they are not about work. They may occur at any time or place. Sometimes they are announced and open to the public.

Sometimes they are between two people. Sometimes they have a purpose; sometimes they don't. Often, the purpose is simply to have fun, to relax, and to kick back a little. We will talk more about socializing at work in a chapter appendix.

3. *Work* meetings are those that are conducted at work, during work hours, about work issues, with work people. These meetings lack the structured, planned elements of formal meetings. They may occur after the normal work hours or include outsiders who bring a special expertise to the meeting, but they are clearly meetings called to deal with work-related topics. Work meetings can be formal or informal.

Communication skills are required in all types of meetings but there may be different kinds of speaking going on in each category. You must know the differences and speak accordingly. It could be a disaster for your job or career if you mix or match inappropriately. Unfortunately, there are no clear-cut, 100 percent foolproof rules. This is because the categories—formal, informal, work, and social—are frequently mixed or mislabeled. Or meetings that are planned, announced, and even conducted as one category can switch to another category without notice. This can even happen mid-meeting. In fact, you will encounter people who purposely mislabel meetings. What is presented as a formal meeting can easily change to an informal meeting. What is announced as a social meeting may well include serious business. An informal meeting may well produce very formal results. Categories are also fluid. A golf game or dinner at a nice restaurant, both of which seem social, may be the settings for conducting very formal business. Even a casual walk through the hallway or a conversation in the washroom can be much more formal than it may appear. So don't be fooled, be ready.

Ask yourself, "Is this meeting formal, informal, work, social?" Then plan and speak accordingly. All of the other tips, techniques, and skills regarding business speaking that are found in this book will apply when speaking at meetings. Take these techniques and modify them to fit the type of meeting where you'll be speaking. For instance, at an informal, social meeting, you may use more humor, more assimilation, more slang. You may even speak faster or with less organization. At a formal meeting, on the other hand, you should speak more clearly, more deliberately, with more carefully organized thoughts. You will have to be the judge of how much change is appropriate for the setting. Remember, however, that all of these are *business* meetings.

Agenda and Purpose

Meetings serve many purposes. You may never know all the purposes for a meeting. There may be an announced purpose, but there may also be an unannounced purpose. In fact, there may be as many unannounced purposes as there are participants in the meeting. When participants pursue an unannounced purpose, this is often referred to as having a *hidden agenda*. Some items being discussed at the meeting make up the published agenda. They are the topics that everyone knows about. Other topics may be private and known to only a few or even known to only one person—these are part of the hidden agenda. You may also have someone you're trying to impress, or something you're trying to find out during the meeting, and you may not want to make that public knowledge; that is *your* hidden agenda. Sometimes a hidden agenda can distract or even block the functioning of the meeting. So always be aware of the presence of hidden agendas. They aren't necessarily negative, but they can be.

There are two main purposes for meetings. One is *information* and the other is *problem solving*. Information meetings are aimed at either *giving* information—for example, briefings, quarterly progress reports, and project updates—or *getting* information—for example, brainstorming, investigations, and idea development. Speaking at meetings is easier if you know which purpose is being pursued. However, don't forget hidden agendas. What may be announced as a problem-solving meeting may actually be an idea-generating meeting for some participants.

We suggest that you take the meeting on head first! If it's announced as a problem-solving meeting, be prepared to do that. Here are a few guidelines for speaking at information and problem-solving meetings.

Information Meetings

1. Ask both general and specific questions.
2. Ask people to clarify anything you don't understand.
3. Be prepared to contribute information, ideas, and opinions.
4. Be prepared to admit when you don't know something.
5. Offer to help research information and ideas that no one seems prepared to handle.
6. Be a good listener.
7. Use paraphrasing to both ensure your accuracy of understanding and to let the speaker know you care enough to pay attention.
8. Take notes.
9. Help develop follow-up ideas and actions for use after the meeting.

Problem-Solving Meetings

1. State the problem in the form of a question.
2. Be sure the problem question is stated fairly and not slanted toward any particular answer.

3. Ask lots of questions.
4. Be open-minded during the problem-solving session.
5. Think the problem through before the meeting.
6. Listen carefully to everyone's ideas.
7. Be aware that while solving one problem, other problems may be identified.
8. Invite and involve anyone who may have ideas, information, or influence on the problem.
9. Give your opinion and ideas based on the available information.
10. Use the following six-step problem-solving technique.

Six-Step Problem-Solving Technique

Step 1 *Introduce the problem.* Be sure the problem is stated clearly. It may be helpful to introduce the participants and set the ground rules, such as time limits. It may also be helpful to provide a brief history of the problem, what brought you to this meeting, and what you expect to accomplish.

Step 2 *Define the terms.* Briefly define each word in the problem topic questions. Do not assume that participants "know what that means" or "everybody understands that." This is such an important step in the technique that you may find disagreement and discussion over definitions. This is quite appropriate. It is very important to the overall solution that everyone clearly define terms *before* proceeding to the next step.

Step 3 *Analyze the problem.* This is the information-gathering step. Ask the who, what, when, where, why, and how questions. Ask participants to contribute any information they can. This step calls for information, not answers. When ideas are repeated, or there are long periods of silence, it's time to move to the next step.

Step 4 *Suggest solutions to the problem.* Go around the room and ask each participant to suggest a solution. It is usually helpful to set a brief time limit for each person's contribution—30 seconds or so is sufficient. The point is to hear all the suggested solutions before beginning any discussion of each solution. Ask participants not to give examples, evidence, or justification for their solution, but just to give the solution; then move to the next step.

Step 5 *Compare solutions to the problem.* Each solution can be dissected and compared with the others. This is frequently the most time-consuming step, when participants attempt to persuade one another. When positions become hardened, when ideas and opinions get repeated, when long pauses occur, or when people get edgy, irritable, or impatient, it's time to move to the next step.

Step 6 *Decide on a solution.* Take a vote—majority rules. Try to be specific about the wording of the solution. Does it answer the question that was posed as the problem in Step 1?

You will notice that Step 6 in this problem-solving technique does not include a plan for action or implementation. That is a logical next step and is usually handled at the meeting as the next order of business. Use the Leadership Action Plan (LAP) to follow up your problem-solving meetings. The Leadership Action Plan form is used by businesspeople who have multiple layers of tasks and by people involved in implementing problem solutions. This simple form is designed to identify and assign specific steps toward problem solving. You can see an example of the form on the facing page.

The LAP form is divided into three simple sections.

1. *Statement of the problem:* Requires a clear, narrative, brief description of the problem. This description should conclude with the problem question that was developed for use with the six-step problem-solving format.

2. *Statement of the solution:* Requires a clear, narrative, brief description of the solution or answer to the problem question.

3. *Actions:* Requires the specific action to be completed, the name of the person who will do it, and a date by when it is expected to be completed.

Some people like to use the bottom of the page for additional comments, dates for follow-up meetings, review dates, or signatures of appropriate people. All of these are optional.

Now, about *leadership:* It seems that the constant ambition of most people in American business is to advance themselves. Upward mobility is a goal in itself for many people in business. People in leadership positions are admired and respected. Meetings are a great opportunity to earn and exert leadership. This text is not designed to cover leadership characteristics in depth, but the speaking techniques covered here will enhance your leadership style and impressions.

1. Practice active listening skills. We'll cover this in more depth in Chapter 9.

2. Whether you are the appointed or elected leader in a group, or a participant, be sure your speaking behavior is assertive, not aggressive. *Aggressive* speakers totally dominate the meeting. They interrupt; they talk over others; they talk loudly; and they generally invade the space and time of others in the group. *Assertive* speakers state their position clearly, then allow interaction by others. They listen; they speak succinctly; they ask questions; and they generally show interest and respect for others.

3. Be informed on the topic and procedure of the meeting. You don't have to be an expert, but you should have enough information about the topic to keep up with the discussion.

LEADERSHIP ACTION PLAN

Problem:

_____

_____

_____

_____

_____

_____

_____

_____

_____

_____

Solution:

_____

_____

_____

_____

_____

_____

_____

Actions I'll Take:	By	Actions Others Will Take:	By

4. Be both a *content* person and a *process* person. Good leaders are aware of the issues that are important to the content being discussed and are aware of the process being used in the meeting to discuss the content.

5. Ask questions whenever you are in doubt. Don't be ashamed or shy about asking questions—it's a good way to learn. Of course, this doesn't mean you should go into the meeting unprepared. In fact, there may be times when you actually know the answer, but asking the question may help others in the group feel comfortable. They will admire and thank you for having the courage to speak up.

6. Involve people in the meeting. Be the person who helps ensure that everyone has an opportunity to participate. Ask others for their ideas and opinions. Be sure the stronger members don't overpower the less strong members.

7. Summarize periodically as the meeting goes along. This helps you retain a grasp on the content and process of the meeting. In addition, other members will respect and reward your ability to keep ideas and organization in line.

8. Be a problem-solving leader using the six-step technique.

Interviews

The *interview* is a special meeting. In fact, if you don't do well in the interview you may not need to know about the other types of meetings. Here are a few important dos and don'ts on how to be most effective when you go for an interview:

- **Do** inform yourself about the company. Research and understand the type of business where you're applying. What do they do? How do they do it? Who are their customers? What are their future projects? What is this job? Where does it fit in the company? Who am I meeting? Why? Don't go in asking these questions. These are all things that you can and should research *before* the interview. Be informed. It makes you look and feel much more confident.

- **Do** prepare yourself. Be sure you've thought about how you'd like to do the type of work required for this job. How will you feel telling family and friends what your job is? What questions do you want to ask your interviewer? Do you have any minimum or maximum number of hours you'd like to work? What about salary? What is your greatest fear about this job? What are your greatest strengths and weaknesses regarding the technical skills needed for the job?

- **Don't** overdress. Don't underdress, for that matter. Try to visit the business site and dress according to what seems appropriate.

- **Do** be yourself. You have certain strengths that you will want to shine a light on. Identify them clearly and do what you can to communicate them.
- **Do** practice active listening. Establish good eye contact, sit erect, and speak clearly and loudly enough to give an impression of confidence. Respond to questions with simple, direct answers.
- **Don't** be shy about talking about yourself. That's the major value in a personal interview—you have the opportunity to let people get to know you. So don't be shy about discussing your strengths and weaknesses—especially your strengths.
- **Do** use the following self-sell outline. You may be asked, ''Tell me about yourself,'' or ''What would you like us to know about you?'' Deliver the information in the following order:

Self-Sell Outline

1. Make a *can do* statement. Give a clear message of confidence that you are capable of doing the job.
2. Make a *benefit* statement. How will their business benefit by hiring you?
3. Describe your *qualifications*. List the academic or technical training that qualifies you for the job, and relate any other pertinent qualifications.
4. Describe your *workstyle*. Do you work well with people? Are you better working alone? Are you a morning or evening person? Do you have a sense of humor? This type of information and insight is very valuable to interviewers. They often don't know how to ask for it. You can be helpful. Share information about yourself in a polite fashion that shows your flexibility.
5. Suggest *action* to be taken. Volunteer to return for another interview. Volunteer to call or make a special visit to a key person. It may also be useful to request a description of the decision-making process. And, of course, end with a thank you for the opportunity.

Chapter Review

- A business meeting occurs any time two or more people exchange ideas.
- Meetings can occur any time and any place.
- There are four major categories of meetings: formal, informal, work, and social.

- The four categories of meetings are frequently intertwined.
- Interview meetings benefit from your use of the self-sell outline:

  1. Make a can do statement.
  2. Make a benefit statement.
  3. Give your qualifications for the job.
  4. Describe your workstyle clearly.
  5. Suggest an action to take following the interview.

- Be prepared to deal with hidden agendas of participants.
- The two main purposes for meetings are:

  1. Information.
  2. Problem solving.

- Problem-solving meetings benefit from use of the six-step problem-solving technique:

  1. Introduce the problem.
  2. Define terms.
  3. Analyze the problem.
  4. Suggest solutions.
  5. Compare solutions.
  6. Decide on a solution.

Practice Exercises

1. Describe three separate meetings you participated in during the past week. Tell what the purpose was, who the leader was, how the meeting was arranged and conducted, and whether or not the purposes were accomplished.
2. Formulate a problem question pertaining to an unsettling condition in your school. Divide into small groups of four or five participants. Use the six-step problem-solving technique to solve the problem.
3. Evaluate the leadership you've seen in a community meeting. Describe the assertive versus aggressive behaviors of the leader. Discuss any hidden agendas that seemed to be present.
4. Divide into groups of four or five participants. Do not assign a leader. Ask a question similar to the following of each group: ''What are the three most important characteristics required to be elected President?'' Tape-record a 15-minute meeting. Play it back and analyze the role of leadership and/or how it emerged. Was the six-step problem-solving format used? What order was followed? What would have improved the process of that meeting?

Quick Quiz

1. What is a meeting?
2. What are the four major categories of business meetings?
3. During an interview meeting, what is the first step in the self-sell outline?
4. Generally speaking, what are the two main purposes for a meeting?
5. In the six-step problem-solving format, what is Step 2?
6. What does Step 2 of the problem-solving format mean?
7. In the six-step problem-solving format, when are solutions suggested?
8. To enhance your leadership at meetings, what kind of listening should be used?
9. Explain the concept of the *hidden agenda*.
10. Why is it a good idea to set a time limit on Step 4 of the six-step problem-solving format?

CHAPTER APPENDIX

SOCIAL INTERACTION: A SPECIAL TYPE OF COMMUNICATION

Business etiquette is *not* the focus of this appendix. However, we would be quite remiss as speech coaches if we did not include a few guidelines on etiquette. Much of the speaking you will do in a business setting will look like social interacting, but don't be fooled. Business is business. Always be prepared to conduct your communication in the most professional manner possible. Here is a list of the most important dos and don'ts we've learned over the years:

1. **Do** be honest. Tell the truth. Don't lie. This doesn't mean that you must tell someone that his sweater makes him look fat, or that her new hairstyle accentuates her big nose. Being honest doesn't mean being rude. If you can't say anything nice, don't say anything, just smile politely.
2. **Do** accentuate the positive. Be a person who speaks, thinks, and acts toward others with the attitude that the glass is half full, not half empty.
3. **Don't** be late for meetings.
4. **Don't** make any commitment that you can't keep. Sometimes unexpected things happen and even your best intentions get sidetracked. Apologize and do your best. But think ahead, and don't make promises you can't fulfill.

5. **Do** be a good, active listener.

6. **Do** smile frequently. Find a reason or make one. Everyone will respect you for it.

7. **Don't** gossip. It's fine to discuss issues, even sensitive issues pertaining to co-workers. But don't repeat rumors, cast aspersions on people, pry into personal lives, or otherwise be a busybody.

8. **Do** show sincere concern for others. Express an interest in their interests and create opportunities for people to talk about themselves and their interests. You be the listener.

9. **Do** ask questions. This is effective in both formal business meetings and as informal social settings at work. Learn the difference between open-ended questions and closed-ended questions; then use each appropriately. An open-ended question in one that cannot be answered in one or two words. Open-ended questions begin with how, why, when, who, what, or where. They encourage participation and contribution by the other person. A closed-ended question is one that can be answered by one or two words. Closed-ended questions begin with did, is, can, will, do, or would. These questions do not encourage interaction or the exchange of ideas or information.

10. **Don't** tell insensitive jokes. These are sexist jokes, racist jokes, or other kinds of stories that make fun of other people. You may get a quick laugh, but you'll definitely get a longer lasting reputation as a person of little sensitivity and poor taste.

11. **Do** develop a personable style, not a personal style, of interacting with others. Know where to draw the line about what topics are too personal to be discussed at work. Remember to draw your own lines. What is too personal for you? Being personable is a professional skill that includes all of the speaking techniques we've discussed plus being sensitive to what is appropriate in a work environment.

12. **Don't** use foul language. Locker room language, street talk, or whatever you call it, it's bad news when used in a business environment. Remember, ''Profanity is the effort of a feeble mind to express itself forcibly.''

13. **Do** be polite and courteous. We know this can get sticky between men and women. Opening doors, pulling out chairs, giving up seats, and helping with coats may seem patronizing and sexist when done by men for women. So be courteous but sensitive.

14. **Do** practice good hygiene. Wash, shave, comb, brush, iron, and change clothing every day, sometimes several times a day. What you look like can speak louder than what you say.

15. **Don't** make the small talk mistake. You often hear people say, ''I hate small talk,'' or ''I'm not very good at small talk.''

Mistake! Small talk is really big talk. Talking about subjects that seem mundane or even inane can be wonderful opportunities to help people feel comfortable with you. Small talk allows people to get acquainted and takes away the pressure to feel productive or practical. Small talk is a chance to be exploratory, unorganized, and fanciful. You'll show a willingness to hear other people on their own terms without the judgmental factors that accompany normal business discussions. Learn how to do it and like it. You'll have as much opportunity to get to know people through small talk as through any other means.

16. **Do** try to meet everyone you work with. We realize that some people are hard to talk to. Try anyway. You'll get a reputation as a friendly person. A good friend of ours who is the director of training at a major research laboratory has a wonderful way of making this approach successful. She ''expects excellence'' in everyone. That is, she finds the good, the friendly, the interesting, the fascinating part of a person and talks to that part.

17. **Do** be self-critical. Try to see and hear yourself as others see and hear you. This is not the same as being self-centered. Being self-critical is an honest attempt to be the best communicator you can be. Be yourself, of course, but be the best speaker and best listener you can be.

Above all:

1. Be honest.
2. Be personable.
3. Be in control of your speaking and listening skills.
4. Be yourself.

Remember, these are the communication skills you'll need in business.

Language and Word Choice

"To communicate ideas, to light a spark that in turn causes people to dream is perhaps the single most important tool a producer can have.
  "Well chosen, passionate words move mountains!"
Vin Di Bona, *President, Vin Di Bona Productions*

Chapter Objectives

After reading this chapter, you will be able to:

1. Understand the importance of language choice in business.
2. Use the 6 Cs of effective language choice: be clear, concise, consistent, colorful, concrete, and correct.
3. Follow basic language choice guidelines.
4. Correct common mispronunciations for more effective speaking.

In this chapter, you will learn that language is a powerful tool in business speaking. The words you choose are building blocks for constructing your thoughts and presenting them to your listeners.

History is filled with the words of men and women, famous and anonymous, that have stirred millions of listeners. In your personal history, you have memories of special words or phrases that were spoken to you and have stayed with you for years. The same is true of you as a speaker. The words you use, and how you construct them to express thoughts, will have a direct impact on your success in business speaking.

This chapter will cover the 6 Cs: techniques for using effective business language. We will also provide examples and ideas for improving your choice of words.

Language Choice: How Can It Help You?

Your language, or word choice, will help your listeners understand and react to your ideas. The opposite can also occur—you can confuse listeners. You must decide what you want to accomplish with your listeners and choose language accordingly. In business speaking, the emphasis is usually on the content of your speech. Do you have anything valuable to say? Speakers often have important information to convey, but the importance is not communicated because of poor word choice or sentence construction. Even when your message isn't critical or urgent, effective use of language can help listeners to see, feel, and identify meaning.

The importance of language choice in business speaking cannot be overstated. We are often asked to identify the ''correctness'' or ''incorrectness'' of words or phrases. In fact, we are asked about the correctness or incorrectness of all of the elements of business speaking. Our answer is always the same: The key is not correct or incorrect, it's effective or ineffective. Use the tools and techniques that will be most effective for you. This does not mean that you should use any words you like. Many listeners are carefully tuned to what they think is correct. We will talk about this in more detail a bit later.

In Chapter 5, on persuasive and informative speaking, we urged you to follow the three Cs: be *clear,* be *concise,* and be *consistent.* We fine-tune the three Cs in this chapter to help you strengthen your control over your language. We'll elaborate on them first, then add three more Cs: be *colorful,* be *concrete,* and be *correct.*

1. Be Clear

Keep your language simple. Use familiar, everyday words. Construct simple declarative sentences. This will be an asset in speaking about difficult or complex subjects, particularly when speaking about technical information to nontechnical people. Remember, what is commonplace language to you may be very uncommon to your listeners. If you are speaking to listeners who are unfamiliar with your topic, you should avoid slang, jargon, and technical wording. Be clear.

Here is an example:

> *Not clear:* Research indicates the product identification coupled with amplification and communication concepts congruent with community mores through simultaneous electronic media exposure will enhance bottom line volume.
> *Clear:* Effective advertising creates profit.

> *Not Clear:* Our thinking leads us to the conclusion that our group effort will not succeed in achieving its goal if management is not supportive of the project.
> *Clear:* We think our group effort will fail if management does not support the project.

2. Be Concise

As Franklin Delano Roosevelt once said, "a good speaker will *be sincere . . . be brief . . . be seated!*"

Business speakers often make the mistake of reading speeches. Written and spoken language should be different. While long, compound, complex sentences can be seen, read, and reread on the printed page for clarity and meaning, those same words and sentences may not be easily heard when uttered only once by a speaker. Be concise.

Several decades earlier, another President Roosevelt reworded a government memo he felt was not concise.

> *Not concise:* Such preparations shall be made as will completely obscure all Federal buildings and non-Federal buildings occupied by the government during an air raid for any period of time from visibility by reason of internal or external illumination. Such obscuration may be obtained either by blackout construction or by termination of the illumination.
> *Concise:* Tell them that in buildings where they have to keep the work going to put something over the windows. And, in buildings where they can let the work stop for a while, turn out the lights.

Here is another example:

> *Not concise:* We believe the issue at hand would benefit by immediate attention to future responses.
> *Concise:* We want action.

3. Be Consistent

Use the same language to refer to the same item each time you mention it. Don't change identifying labels or terms during your speech.

Business speakers frequently make the mistake of changing terminology because they know exactly what is intended. Listeners, however, may not recognize the similarity in terms and can easily become confused or even angry. This is also true when using visuals. Always use the same words in your visual that you use in speaking. Be consistent.

> *Not consistent:* Federal revenue enhancers will affect transportation budgets. Financial requests should reflect these travel taxes.
>
> *Consistent:* Federal travel taxes will affect transportation budgets. Financial requests should reflect these travel taxes.
>
> *Not consistent:* A slide *reads*, ''Market **growth** from 1990 to 1995.'' The speaker *says*, ''Here's data on market **proliferation** from 1990 to 1995.''

4. Be Colorful

When we refer to color, we are speaking about words that create an impression or enhance meaning. These are called *color* words. They can change ordinary, straightforward, black-and-white information into colorful and memorable messages. This can be accomplished by using a more varied style of speaking. Almost any word can be a color word. You colorize words by changing the inflection, volume, intensity, or speed used to produce the word. Each colorized word brings a different meaning to the thought. You must decide which words best represent your main thoughts and colorize those words. This will help listeners identify meaning as well as enjoy your speaking. Be colorful.

Here are some examples:

> *Not colorful:* The conference and workshops produced a positive response from the participants.
> *Colorful: Everyone* who attended the sessions had a *great* time.
>
> *Not colorful:* Molly and Tim are both quite talented.
> *Colorful:* Molly *and* Tim are *both quite talented*.

5. Be Concrete

Be specific. Use language that directly expresses your meaning. Don't assume listeners will know what you mean. Tentative language can produce misunderstanding, frustration, and errors. Be concrete.

Here are examples:

> *Not concrete:* I hope I have shown you three reasons for the deficit.
> *Concrete:* I have shown you three reasons for the deficit.
> *Not concrete:* I think I could do this project.
> *Concrete:* I can do this project for you.

One common speaking problem is using nonconcrete, tentative language during business speaking. Here is a list of the most frequently heard words and phrases that we urge you to avoid:

I think.	You know.
I feel.	Kind of.
I hope.	Perhaps.
I guess.	Maybe.
I tend to think.	It seems.
A little.	Sort of.
May or might.	Could.
	Somewhat.

6. Be Correct

It feels strange to say *be correct*. We are normally interested in *being effective*. There are, however, two ways to look at correctness. First, there are people who follow the grammar of our language. They go by the book—the grammar book. A second group of people follows the usage of our language. They go by what's being used on the street. However, slang and profanity are *never* correct or effective in business speaking.

There will always be a bit of the "when in Rome, do as the Romans do" philosophy. It is wise to understand the local habits and dialect or vernacular. This doesn't mean that you should try to speak like the people who live and work in that region or business environment. In fact, local residents may find it offensive if you try to sound like them. Be yourself. It's easier and safer. The point to remember, however, is that rude, crude language, the four-letter, locker room type, gives a very bad impression in a business setting. Naturally, you will always find someone who uses it. As we mentioned in Chapter 6, "Profanity is the effort of a feeble mind to express itself forcibly."

The following are guidelines for a few of the language errors we hear most commonly in business speaking.

1. Agreement in Number

Incorrect: There is many reasons for the decline.

Correct: There are many reasons for the decline.

Incorrect: An insufficient number of workers are the chief cause of the slowdown.

Correct: An insufficient number of workers is the chief cause of the slowdown.

2. Use of Like

Incorrect: Like, it's one of the best tools we have. We like use it for everything. Customers like really like it, too.

Correct: It's one of the best tools we have. We use it for everything. Customers really like it, too.

Like used as in the preceding example is slang. It indicates an immature inability to sound professional. You know, like when a guy's trying to be like, grown up and stuff, and like he uses like big words and stuff. That's like weird like, you know.

Like should not be used before clauses or phrases. Use *as, as if, as though,* or *that.*

Incorrect: I feel like I should attend the meeting.

Correct: I feel that I should attend the meeting.

Incorrect: Like I said before, we can't afford it.

Correct: As I said before, we can't afford it.

Incorrect: She sounds like she's pleased with the report.

Correct: She sounds as if she's pleased with the report.

3. Use of Myself

Myself is a pronoun and should be used to reflect actions—"I learned myself"—or to emphasize—"I sent the letter myself." However, in most other cases, *I* or *me* is correct.

Incorrect: Myself and the committee chair will report the results next week.

Correct: The committee chair and I will report the results next week.

Incorrect: The proposal was delivered to Stefan and myself.

Correct: The proposal was delivered to Stefan and me.

4. Use of Personal Pronouns such as I, Me, Him, Her, Us, and Them

Use *I* when it is the subject of the sentence. Remember to put yourself last—it's the polite thing to do.

Incorrect: Me and Bud attended.

Correct: Bud and I attended.

Use *me* when it is the subject of the sentence or object of a preposition.

Incorrect: Heidi congratulated Ethan and I.

Correct: Heidi congratulated Ethan and me.

Incorrect: The contract is between you and I.

Correct: The contract is between you and me.

Use *they, we, she,* and *he* when they are one of the subjects of the sentence.

Incorrect: Them and you should give the report.

Correct: You and they should give the report.

Use *him, her, us,* and *them* when they are objects of the preposition *to*.

Incorrect: Greg faxed it to Monica and he today.

Correct: Greg faxed it to Monica and him today.

Mispronunciation is also a flagrant and frequent misuse of language. Here is a list of words that we constantly hear being said incorrectly—that is, speakers mispronounce them.

Word	*What We Hear*	*What It Should Be*
Athlete	Ath u leet	Ath leet
Nuclear	Nuc u lar	Nu klee ar
Ask	Aks	Ask
Length	Lenth	Length
Library	Libary	Li brary
Technical	Tetnichal	Tech nical
Recognize	Rec u nize	Rec og nize
Probably	Probly	Pro bab ly
Picture	Pitch er	Pik cher

We wish we could make this easy for you by providing more side-by-side, good and bad, right and wrong, effective and ineffective examples. It isn't possible. Every speech must be given and heard within the unique set of circumstances existing at the time of the speech. Choosing words for use in effective business speaking requires that you understand the circumstances present at that time. This is why Martin Luther King, Jr.'s enormously powerful ''I Have a Dream'' speech doesn't have the same impact today as it did when originally delivered. This is why John Kennedy's ''Ask not what your country can do for you'' speech was so meaningful initially, but has a very different impact today. Yes, these great speeches will always be meaningful. The words still stir passion in people. The messages are still strong, but times are different, listeners are different, the settings in which we hear these speeches are different. All these differences alter the effectiveness of a speech.

We can generalize about how to choose words, and give you guidelines, but only you can select and use the most effective words in a given business speech.

Chapter Review

- Words are building blocks for your ideas.
- Use the six Cs when choosing language.
    - Be clear.
    - Be concise.
    - Be consistent.
    - Be colorful.
    - Be concrete.
    - Be correct.

Practice Exercises

1. Choose two different TV commercials and describe the words used according to the six Cs.
2. Compare and contrast a radio commercial with a TV commercial. Emphasize any differences in word choice when video is involved.
3. Divide in small groups of four to six people. Assign two members of the groups to prepare a three-to-five minute speech on the same topic. Tell one speaker to use language that is likely to be heard in a formal business setting. The other speaker should use casual language. Ask the listeners to evaluate the effectiveness of each speaker's word choice.
4. Listen to a live or recorded speech delivered by a politician. Try to reword the same speech. What other words could be used to create the same ideas? Why do you think the politician chose those particular words?

Quick Quiz

1. What are the six Cs to keep in mind when choosing language?
2. Give eight examples of tentative language.
3. Why should the words on your visuals match the words in your speech?

4. What should be used before clauses or phrases instead of the commonly misused word *like*?
5. What two words should not be substituted for *myself* as a pronoun reflecting action?
6. List at least five words that are frequently mispronounced.
7. What are color words?
8. When relating technical information to nontechnical individuals, the key is to be _____ .
9. When speaking about difficult or complex matters, how should you construct your sentences?
10. What is the difference between grammar and usage?

Using Nonverbal Communication

"Effective communication can make the difference between the success or failure of a business executive. Communication takes many forms—it goes beyond standard oral and written presentation. Of critical importance to one's success is personal presentation. In business, we are often judged by a first impression: The way we look, the way we speak, the way we shake hands. That first impression may serve as an everlasting impression, so make it your best."
Lesley Berkovitz, *Vice President, Human Resources, Sunglass Hut*

Chapter Objectives

After reading this chapter, you will be able to:

1. Understand the basics of clothing as nonverbal communication.
2. Recognize the use of facial expressions in business speaking.
3. Use eye contact effectively.
4. Use body language appropriately in business speaking.

As a business speaker, you communicate over two channels at the same time—audio and video. Everything your listeners hear is on the audio channel and everything your listeners see is on the video channel. In this chapter, we will devote attention to the video channel. After all, except for telephone speaking, the first thing your listeners do is look at you. How are you dressed? Do your clothes fit? Do they match? What style are your clothes? How do you move in the room? How do you use your body to communicate? Listeners look at body movement, eye contact, facial expression, and gestures. All of these nonverbal aspects of you are ''speaking'' a loud, nonverbal language. They are an important part of your business-speaking skills.

This chapter will review the most important information on nonverbal behaviors. We will introduce two important guidelines for controlling nonverbal behavior. Finally, we will briefly discuss those elements of nonverbal behavior that are not directly controlled by you but that have a direct impact on your message.

Dress

Clothing, or dress style, is often the first thing your listeners tune in to. Some businesses have formal dress codes—you are told what is appropriate to wear. For example, many businesses regard short shorts, cutoffs, and miniskirts as inappropriate, or prohibit tank tops on men or women. Others require ties for men or stockings for women. Some of these dress codes are related to safety or health factors. Some are designed to project or protect a particular business image. Businesses that have formal, written dress codes are becoming less and less common. But don't be fooled. Every business has an informal, unwritten dress code. Listeners may not always admit it, but they are influenced by what you wear.

This is not a dress-for-success book. There are many of those and we recommend that you find a good one. At least familiarize yourself with the broad thinking of the day. For the most part, those books are merely one person's opinion, but you may find some pertinent information in them.

Be comfortable with your clothing style. Don't simply wear what everyone else is wearing—be yourself. That doesn't mean, however, that you should ignore the signals and styles of your boss, your customers, or those in your business who have done well. They all know something about what is appropriate. For example, if your boss and others in management positions wear suits, that is a signal that you, too, should consider wearing a suit. It may not be necessary to wear the same color, texture, or style as they do, but a suit would be better than jeans and a sweater.

Don't follow the styles you see on TV or in the movies and magazines. Those fashions are usually overdone and too fancy for average business attire. If you are in doubt about whether a particular look is appropriate, it probably isn't.

Always be respectful in your clothing style. Your dress says something about how you regard and value your listeners. If you dress down and dirty, or casual and carefree, your listeners may well feel that that is your opinion of them. Whenever you are in doubt about this judgment, and your appearance is important, make your decisions based on the normal appearance of your listeners. Show that you respect them by dressing nicely. They may not say anything about it. They may not even consciously notice it. However, they will definitely notice it and may even say something if your dress is inappropriate.

In addition, be very careful with jewelry and other accessories. Simpler is safer. Don't go crazy with rings, watches, bracelets, brooches, earrings, noserings, and hairpieces. We know these things are all in vogue these days. Be careful. You will be working with many people whose fashion taste may come from a totally different generation or culture. They won't appreciate your stylishness. Also, be careful about choosing fancy pens, pencils, briefcases, handbags, and shoulder bags. Remember, simpler is safer.

Facial Expression and Eye Contact

Two of the most visible, flexible, and powerful nonverbal tools you have as a speaker are eye contact and facial expression. In fact, they are among the most powerful tools your *listeners* have, as well. Listeners pick up cues about the speaker's meaning and intent, and even judge honesty and love, by a speaker's facial expressions and eye contact. We're sure you've heard the sayings, "The eyes are the windows of the soul," or "What a poker face." There is no doubt that both speaker and listener use facial expressions and eye contact to send and interpret messages — in other words, to communicate.

Facial Expressions

Let's look at facial expressions first.

Smile!   Wow! What an effective tool for helping people feel comfortable with you. A smile is a natural and friendly gesture that often prompts others to smile at you. Do you realize that humans may be the only animals on earth who bear their teeth in friendship. People like smiling. Obviously you shouldn't smile at inappropriate times. Smiling would seem inappropriate or ineffective with certain serious, sad, or controversial subjects. You'll have to decide for yourself when these times occur. Be sensitive to the fact that some people may misinterpret a smile. Perhaps you've gotten into some trouble by smiling at people who thought you were flirting with them, or mocking them, so be careful in these situations.

Learn to smile. Get in front of a mirror and practice. Look at your smile on videotape. Is it big enough? Can it be seen? Facial bone structure varies greatly. Many of us haven't been blessed with the Hollywood look. Men, be careful that your mustache doesn't hide your smile. Women, be careful that your lipstick doesn't overwhelm your natural beauty. A nice smile can go a long way in making you and your listeners comfortable.

Other Facial Expressions   Frowning and nodding are often uncontrollable behaviors in speakers, but you can learn to control both of these. They are often indicators to another speaker that you agree, disagree, or are pleased or unhappy about a particular point. They are strong sign language "words" about your innermost feelings.

Facial expressions of joy, excitement, concern, doubt, and so on can also strongly reinforce the words and content of your speaking. They also make you a more interesting speaker to listen to. Take the story of a local TV weatherman. His boss said that viewers didn't find him passionate and enthusiastic enough about the weather. So among other things, he practices in front of the mirror. He is learning how to strengthen and control the dozens of muscles in his face. He may look strange standing in front of the mirror or video camera making faces, but he's learning how to "show" the real passion and enthusiasm he has for weather. Watch other speakers, watch TV personalities, watch yourself on videotape. You'll quickly see the impact and value of learning to work with your facial expressions.

Eye Contact

Eye contact is extremely important. Have you ever noticed how many human behaviors and attitudes get conveyed by eye contact? There are at least five different words that begin with the letter G describing eye contact and accompanying behavior and attitudes:

Gaze	Love, affection, friendliness
Glare	Hate, fear, threat
Gawk	Snoop, curious, intrude
Google	Wide-eyed, silly, playful
Glower	Anger, warning, intimidate

Eye contact is generally considered to be the most important visual reinforcer a speaker has. Listeners like to be looked at. This is particularly true in persuasive business speaking. The American business culture relies heavily on the "look 'em straight in the eye" approach.

Generally speaking, eye contact should be a controlled speaking behavior. Don't stare at people, yet don't be too fleeting. That may sound contradictory, so here are three tips for effective eye contact while speaking:

1. Hold eye contact for approximately one to three seconds, then move on to someone else. If you're in a deep and serious one-on-one conversation, the time could easily double or triple.

2. Use the X-Y-Z technique. That means move eye contact around the room in an X, Y, or Z pattern. Think of yourself as drawing one of these letters with your eyes.

3. Move your eye contact everywhere—don't look at only one or two people. This is a common mistake. You may find textbooks on speaking that urge you to "find a friendly face in the audience and make eye contact with and talk to that person." Don't do it. It's nice to feel comfortable with your listeners. However, if you get too comfortable and have too much eye contact with one listener, you'll lose the others. They will feel rejected and ignored. Be careful of this common mistake. Move eye contact around.

Don't Send Mixed Messages

Be sure your eye contact and facial expressions match the words and content of your speaking. This is an easy mistake to make. During the 1988 presidential campaign, this was a problem for Michael Dukakis. He had the habit of saying how happy he was, how pleased he was, how excited he was about a subject, but then shaking his head from side to side "showing" an unhappy attitude. Combine this head movement with his heavy dark eyebrows and nonsmiling face and you have a mixed message. We all know what that did for Dukakis. Be careful. Be aware of both your audio and video messages. Don't send mixed messages.

Body Language

Body movement and hand gestures are what we usually consider body language. As you're learning, facial expressions, eye contact, and even dress must be included under the term *body language*. Body movement includes posture, sitting, standing, and walking. Hand gestures include both hand and arm movement. Many years ago, speakers were taught very specific rules about body movement and hand gestures. Speech coaches were rigid about the posturing of the wrist or leg during a speech. This accounts for the very posed and stiff-looking posture on the statues of famous people that we see in parks and museums throughout the country. Fortunately, the more natural approach is now in vogue.

There are still some generally accepted dos and don'ts concerning body language. Here are a few:

- **Don't** slouch when standing to speak. It gives a sloppy appearance and impression.
- **Do** stand up straight and face your listeners directly. It gives the appearance and impression of interest and sincerity.
- **Don't** pace back and forth in front of your listeners. It gives the appearance of nervousness and uncertainty.

- **Do** walk slowly, two or three steps at a time, stopping to talk for a minute or two between movements. This gives the appearance of control and confidence.
- **Don't** gesture below the waist or at your side. It looks weak and unassertive.
- **Do** gesture at or above the waist. It looks stronger and more confident.
- **Don't** bend your fingers when counting or enumerating. It looks weak.
- **Do** keep fingers straight and pointed upward when counting or enumerating. It looks stronger.
- **Don't** be a band leader who gestures on almost every word, usually with the same gesture. It is distracting and a sign of nervousness.
- **Do** gesture to emphasize your important points. It helps listeners identify and accept important ideas.
- **Don't** gesture broadly in a small conversation or sitting at a meeting. It looks unnatural and aggressive.
- **Do** gesture in these small conversations and meetings by using about half the space you'd cover in a more formal standing presentation. It looks and feels more natural and comfortable.

Beyond Body Language

The American business environment is rapidly expanding to reflect a broader international marketplace. Therefore, it is increasingly important to be sensitive to cultural diversity and its relationship to communication complexity. Understanding a spoken language such as Spanish, Italian, German, or Chinese is extremely valuable, though few of us master these. But perhaps even more valuable is cross-cultural understanding of the nonverbal habits and patterns of other cultures. There are many books dealing with business etiquette and cultural differences. You would be well served to find one you like and use it to become familiar with the particular cultural patterns relating to your business environment.

"Speaking" with nonverbal language can require almost as much attention as the actual speaking itself. We could devote an entire book to this subject—many people have. As we said in the beginning of this chapter, it's a good idea to check out the local bookstore or library for a book on dressing for success that you might enjoy. For our purposes, allow us to leave you with two simple yet powerful guidelines:

1. Be yourself. Dress, move, and gesture in ways that are natural and comfortable to you. Don't try to *be* anything you're not.
2. Don't do anything that attracts unfavorable attention to yourself. If you're not sure whether your dress or actions attract "negative" attention, ask a friend, coach, or colleague. If you're still not sure, modify your habits.

Chapter Review

- You are constantly communicating over both audio and video channels.
- The first thing listeners judge about you is your appearance.
- Dress comfortably and appropriately for your business.
- Read a good dress-for-success book.
- Smiling is a very powerful tool for speakers.
- Frowning and nodding should be voluntary, at appropriate times, not involuntary.
- Don't send mixed messages.
- Hold eye contact an average of one to three seconds per person while speaking.
- Be yourself.
- Don't do anything that calls unfavorable attention to yourself.

Practice Exercises

1. Divide into small groups in class. Take turns expressing your feelings about a national issue by using only three words and nonverbal body language.
2. Choose a TV personality and report to the class on his or her use of nonverbal language.
3. Choose a popular music video. Watch it with the sound turned off. See if you can tell the story of the song by the nonverbal language.
4. Choose any three emotions and practice communicating them through nonverbal language only.
5. Working in a small group, plan a two-minute speech on a subject you feel strongly about. Then ask your coaches to critique the match between audio and video as discussed in this chapter.
6. In a small group, try a one-minute speech using absolutely no nonverbal language. Move only your mouth. This is tougher than it sounds. Ask your group members to stop you when you show any nonverbal behavior.

Quick Quiz

1. What is the difference between audio and video channels of communication?
2. What is a good rule of thumb for dress and appearance?

3. Which is more important to control, clothing or jewelry?
4. Which facial expression is almost always positive and safe to use?
5. What is a mixed message?
6. What is a good average time to hold eye contact?
7. What is the X-Y-Z technique?
8. Should you establish and hold eye contact with one friendly face and talk to that person?
9. Why is gesturing at every word or phrase in a speech a particularly bad speaking habit?
10. ''Be yourself'' is one of two important nonverbal language guidelines. What's the other one?

9 Learning to Listen

A wise old owl lived in an oak;
The more he saw the less he spoke.
The less he spoke
the more he heard:
Why can't we all be like that bird?
Anonymous

"Listening as it applies to effective communication, is a learned ability. We are born with the sense of hearing but each of us must continually improve and enhance our listening skills to ensure that we 'receive' messages as they are intended by the 'sender.'"
Richard Kalagher, *President, First Eastern Mortgage Corporation*

Chapter Objectives

After reading this chapter, you will be able to:

1. Understand the difference between hearing and listening in a business context.
2. Recognize and eliminate passive listening characteristics.
3. Use active listening skills to improve your overall concentration and understanding.
4. Make the connection between active listening and effective speaking.

This chapter will provide many of you with your first formal lesson in listening. Most of us have had informal lessons in listening since we were children. We learned to listen for information, or pleasure, or because we were told to listen—or else. It was a true live-and-learn experience. In this chapter, we will discuss the value of listening in business. We will also teach you the difference between active and passive listening. Finally, you will learn five important techniques for becoming an effective listener in business.

Hearing versus Listening

The wise old owl who is quoted at the beginning of this chapter certainly had the right idea. Good listeners do learn a lot. They learn *what* people speak about and they learn *how* people speak. Throughout your experiences you have already tuned in to both what and how people speak. How many times have you heard someone say something, and then commented, "It's not *what* he said that concerns me—it's *how* he said it." Or "I can tell by the *way* she's speaking that she doesn't really like the idea. It's not in her words; it *how* she's saying them." This same sensitivity will be helpful in business. Your listening skills will help you understand more precisely what a customer is concerned about or what your boss really means. Consequently, you will be able to react in the most appropriate manner.

Hearing and listening are not the same process. *Hearing* is the physical act of sound striking the eardrum. *Listening* is differentiating among those sounds. Hearing is an involuntary and reflexive act. Listening is a voluntary and initiative act. As you read these words, you are hearing sounds in the room or outside the building. You are probably hearing an air-conditioning system or a furnace, or voices in the hallway. Perhaps you are hearing street traffic or an airplane. Hearing these sounds simply means that the sounds are striking your eardrum. It's not until you focus on these sounds that you are actually listening to them. Now that we've mentioned them, do you *hear* the sounds around you? Are you *listening* to them? In a business environment, you will *hear* many sounds that could demand your attention.

Listening behavior is either active or passive. *Passive* listeners do not give full attention to the speaker. Passive listening is characterized by looking away from the speaker, thinking about other subjects while listening, or perhaps engaging in another activity such as writing a letter, or reading an article, or even carrying on a conversation with a second speaker. Passive listening means not concentrating on the speaker's message with your full capacity. It is widely accepted that passive listening is not as beneficial or productive as active listening. However, as many parents know, many children can study or do homework while "listening" to the radio. These children may say, "but I think better when the radio is on," or "I can't concentrate without the radio on." A whole generation of young people has listened passively to the radio while "concentrating" on something else. This may work for children—but passive listening is *not* appropriate in a business setting.

Active listening gives full attention to the speaker. Active listeners establish good eye contact with the speaker and give the speaker nonverbal indications such as nodding to indicate that they are paying attention. Active listening may mean taking notes on the speaker's topic or asking related questions. Active listeners become involved with the speaker *and* the topic.

Active Listening Skills

To become a better active listener, practice the following five techniques.

1. Get Ready to Listen

We know this sounds simple, but it isn't. When listening really matters to you—for instance, when you're called to a meeting with your boss, or when you're receiving instructions on how to operate machinery—you must get physically and psychologically ready to listen. You should have note-taking materials available. You may need to turn off the radio, stand or sit more erect, and make an agreement with yourself that you'll stop whatever else you're doing and *get ready* for this listening experience.

2. Pay Attention to the Speaker

This also sounds simple, but again, it isn't. It is very easy to be distracted by what the speaker is wearing, or by another person in the room, an unusual piece of furniture, or artwork. To *pay attention,* concentrate on how the speaker has organized the subject, identify and follow her theme, main points, and supporting points. Make an agreement with yourself that you'll purposely *not* think about other subjects while listening to the speaker.

3. Control Biases While Listening

This may be the most difficult thing you'll have to do as an effective listener. To *control biases* is almost unnatural. We all have biases, many of which we aren't even aware of. For instance, if you think flowered ties are ugly and only stupid people wear them, that's a bias! If your boss shows up at a staff meeting wearing a flowered tie, you'd better control that bias and help yourself listen to his message. As human beings, we have biases of many kinds relating to race, religion, gender, and sports, among others. Be brutally honest with yourself and learn to control your biases.

4. Pick up Cue Words

Cue words are words that speakers use as clues to the meaning and organization of their thoughts. These words and phrases can be particular to a speaker, a particular company, or a culture. Some of the more common cue words used in business are:

Cue Words	Common Meaning
Bottom line.	Cost, final decision.
Run it by.	Get approval.
Rat hole.	Line of pursuit with no value.
Blow it up.	Expand on this idea.
In the ballpark.	Within possibility.
Ducks in a row.	Everyone in agreement.
In the pipeline.	Making it's way through the system.
On board.	In agreement.
Ramp up.	Preparation time.

5. Paraphrase What You've Heard

Repeat back to the speaker what you understand was said. Use your own words and do not attempt to give back every detail. There is a difference between being able to *paraphrase* and parroting. Paraphrasing is repeating the speaker's thoughts in your own words. Parroting is repeating the speaker's thoughts using the speaker's exact words. When you paraphrase well, you tell the speaker that you were a good listener, plus you receive an instant check on the accuracy of what you heard. Naturally, you shouldn't do this every time the speaker completes a thought, or with every speaker. Be reasonable and paraphrase when appropriate.

From Active Listener to Effective Speaker

Speakers are aware of active and passive listeners. They notice whether listeners seem to be paying attention. Effective speakers look for cues of active and passive listening, then adjust their speaking accordingly. We recall an incident in school in a class on Effective Communication. The professor was a boring speaker, so we tried an experiment in active and passive listening. The entire class of 10 students agreed to do the following: Each time the instructor walked to the left of the lectern, we would all give passive listening cues such as staring out the window, doodling, yawning, opening other books, checking our watches, and smiling at each other. Each time the professor walked to the right of the lectern, we would all give active listening cues such as good eye contact, facing the professor, taking notes, nodding appropriately, and asking pertinent questions. The class members did this consistently for three classes. By the end of the fourth class, the professor never passed the lectern to the left. He stayed on the right side of the lectern where he received all positive and active listening reactions. Active listening works.

It's simple—the more you are able to follow the topics under discussion at a meeting, and the better you understand what a speaker is talking about, the more prepared you will be to speak. Active listening makes good business sense.

Chapter Review

- Listening and hearing are not the same process.
- Listening is a voluntary and controlled activity.
- Passive listening gives negative signals to the speaker.
- Active listening gives positive signals to the speaker and others.
- Active listening includes good eye contact, attentive body language, concentration, and response to the speaker.
- Five important techniques for effective active listening are:

  1. Get ready to listen.
  2. Pay attention to the speaker.
  3. Control biases that block listening.
  4. Pick up cue words used by the speaker.
  5. Paraphrase periodically to check for accuracy and to let the speaker know you're tuned in.

Practice Exercises

1. Check your own listening habits. Keep a personal journal for three days noting whether you speak more or listen more in the course of conversation, classes, and at home with your friends and family.
2. Share examples with your classmates of good and bad listening habits that you observed. Be sure to indicate how you could tell the difference.
3. Listen to a radio commercial. Immediately turn off the radio and try to write down as much of it as you can. This will test your *paraphrasing* skills. Don't parrot!
4. Write a list of habits that get in the way of your own active, effective listening. Share the list with a partner and brainstorm solutions.
5. Engage in a 10-minute conversation with two classmates. Ask a third classmate to observe the listening behaviors of each person. Then rotate roles in the group and do it again.

Quick Quiz

1. Is listening a voluntary or involuntary act?
2. How does hearing differ from listening?
3. Approximately what percentage of the workday does the average person spend listening?
4. Is active or passive listening characterized by eye contact with the speaker?
5. What does "get ready to listen" mean?
6. What is the purpose of cue words?
7. Why is paraphrasing an important skill in relation to listening?
8. Why are cue words important for the listener to pick up?
9. What is the most important result of paying attention?
10. List at least two examples of passive listening.

Effective Telephone Skills

"Those of us who live daily in the hi-tech world are constantly reminded of the hi-touch need to communicate verbally so that we may effectively transfer the information of science."
Susan Colcock, *Director of Training, MIT, Lincoln Laboratory*

Chapter Objectives

After reading this chapter, you will be able to:

1. Understand the crucial role of the telephone as a *business* machine.
2. View business telephone calls as opportunities to increase your company's positive image.
3. Learn the most important rules of making and taking general business calls.
4. Handle upset callers and develop an excellent phone manner.

You are entering the business world during an age of incredible technological growth. Business is rapidly becoming technology-dependent. However, there is one business machine that stands apart from all the others. It is probably the most powerful, productive, and important machine in any business. Most businesses couldn't function without it. Not only that, but workers love it so much that they even have one at home. In fact, most workers have several of these machines at home. People just love this machine! We even give them as gifts to our children and grandparents. We'd do anything for these machines. We'll stop whatever else we're doing just to respond to one of these machines. If we're speaking to other people, even in a serious and intimate manner, we'll stop to respond to this machine. We'll jump out of the tub, run in from the yard, wake up from a sound sleep just so we can respond to this magnificent machine. We are indeed dependent on, in love with, and slaves to the *telephone!*

This chapter covers your relationship with and use of the telephone as a business machine. We will discuss how you present your company's image over the phone and we will provide guidelines for effective telephone use and developing a good phone manner.

You and Your Phone

No machine has had a greater impact on human interaction than the telephone. It is second only to direct speech as a means of communicating feelings, fears, and ideas between people. This is the crux of the love-hate relationship we have with the telephone. It is the only business machine that is found in every office, warehouse, supply room, and board room, and it is also found in just about every home. This may be the root of difficulty many people have using the phone effectively at work—it is one of the only business machines we learn to use at home. When you're at a job interview, you're never asked if you know how to use the phone. You may be asked if you know how to use a particular phone system, but it is expected that you know how to "use" the phone. You probably feel the same way. "Of course I know how to use the phone. After all, I've been using it since I was a child." That is precisely why a problem may arise. When you use the telephone at work, it is a *business* machine, a tool of the trade. You should regard it the same way you regard the other business machines you use. Do not treat the telephone the same at work as you do at home. It may take a concerted effort on your part to start thinking about the telephone as a *business* machine. When you are able to do this, your business speaking on the phone will also change.

Business communication on the phone is in many ways no different than face-to-face business communication. As we've said before, your attitudes are as important as your actions. Try to have a positive attitude toward communication with other people and to regard the telephone as an *opportunity, not an interruption.* We can't count the number of times we've heard people in a customer service position say, ''I wish this phone would stop ringing; maybe then I could get my work done. We'd get more done around here if those customers would stop calling.'' But remember, each time you speak with someone on the phone, you represent your company. You have the opportunity to create a friendly, helpful, professional image and insure a positive attitude in your caller's mind. Take advantage of this opportunity.

Here are a few general guidelines to remember about speaking on the phone:

- Separate personal and professional phone time. Unless otherwise authorized by your boss, you shouldn't be making or receiving personal calls during work hours. Some businesses permit a specific number of personal calls during the workday. When this is permitted, be sure to keep your personal calls short—less than five minutes each.

- Don't take it personally when people are abusive on the phone. Usually they are upset about a professional or business issue and are taking it out on you. They really don't mean it personally. Even if they do, don't take it personally! Be above that. Protect yourself from the stress of taking things too personally over the phone. Keep control.

- Sound enthusiastic and energetic over the phone. Speak loudly enough to be heard by someone who may be sitting 10 feet away. Speak very clearly. Be sure to articulate all the sounds in each word. Don't mumble! Speak somewhat quickly rather than somewhat slowly. Reread Chapter 3, Speaking Clearly. With no visual enhancers such as eye contact, facial expressions, and gestures, your vocal variety and speech clarity are critical. Smile while you speak. Your mouth and lip positioning will create the sound of a friendly smile for the listener.

- Be a good listener. Take notes. Ask questions. Review periodically. Paraphrase frequently. All of these techniques help your understanding. They also help the caller know you are being attentive. Reread Chapter 9, Learning to Listen.

- Be aware that a call *you* place may be considered an interruption. Always ask, ''Do you have the time to speak with me now?'' or a similar question. This is a sign of respect for the receiver of your call.

- Don't eat while on the phone. It seems almost silly to say this, it is so obvious. The sounds of chomping and slurping are most annoying, disrespectful, and unprofessional.

- Don't speak longer than one minute without allowing the person on the other end to participate. Ask for information. Ask for an opinion. Simply stop talking to permit the other person to speak.

- Always be polite and courteous. Say "please" and "thank you" whenever appropriate. We know this sounds very basic, but these courtesies make a big difference to the other person.
- Remember, the telephone presents an opportunity, not an interruption.

Here are a few examples of appropriate and inappropriate phrases:

Do Say	*Don't Say*
How *may* I help you?	*Can* I help you?
May I ask you to hold?	Hold please.
What company are you with?	Where are you calling from?
One moment, please.	Just a second.
He/she is not available. May I help you?	He/she isn't here, or he/she can't come to the phone now.
Thank you for holding.	Silence . . .
Thank you for waiting. May I ask who you are holding for?	Who are you waiting for?
May I ask who's calling?	Who's calling?
Thank you for calling, bye.	OK. Bye.

Making Calls

You will make some calls that are serious, some that are complex, and some that are commonplace. No matter what type of call you are making, here are a few pointers:

1. Have a Plan

Always think about the call *before* you make it. Ask yourself these basic planning questions:

- Why am I calling?
- Who am I calling?
- How long should it take?
- What is my desired outcome?

2. Be Prepared

Have notes, files, or other materials you may need with you. Make the call when you can speak without interruptions.

3. Plan Your Greeting

In your greeting, be sure to include the appropriate information that will enable the answerer to be helpful.

> "Hello. This is Mike Formicone. May I speak to Roy Bilger please?"

Occasionally, it may be necessary to add more information to facilitate the call.

> "Hello. This is Mike Formicone. May I speak to someone who can help me with a question about costs for international travel?"

The important point is that the person on the other end cannot help unless you are specific about why you are calling. When you do get help, always say "thank you"—unless you get the famous "no response" (click) from the other end. If you do, don't get upset. That person simply hasn't read this book yet. You're using the correct, professional business approach.

4. Select Your Language Carefully

Choose the actual words in your greeting. Don't you react differently to the caller who says, "Is Joe there?" than to the caller who says, "May I speak to Joe, please?" Think about what language fits you, your company, and the nature and spirit of the call.

Here are a few examples:

> "May I talk to Rita Finn?"
> "Hello, may I be connected with Rita Finn, please?"
> "Yo, Rita there?"
> "Hiya, is Rita Finn there?"
> "Hello, may I speak with Rita Finn, please?"

You see what we mean? Each change of a word changes the impression.

5. Don't be a Slavemaster

Understand that people are often slaves to the phone and that your call may be regarded as an interruption. (Not by you, of course—you know that it's an opportunity, not an interruption. But there are still some businesspeople who have yet to learn that.) So if your party does not respond the way you expected, it may be necessary to reintroduce yourself:

> "Hi Perry, this is Catherine calling."

Then, add a sentence very similar to this:

> "Do you have a few minutes to talk?
> "Is this a convenient time to discuss the drawings for the new building?"

Give the other person the opportunity to say that it is a bad time or that he or she is not prepared to discuss that issue now. This approach is designed to show respect for the other person's time. It's a polite and professional technique.

6. Conclude Courteously

When your business has been completed, always thank the other person for his or her help. Say something like this:

> "Thanks for your help, Barney. I really appreciate it."
> "This has been helpful. Thank you for your time and assistance."
> "I realize this took time to complete and I want to thank you."

7. Leave a Meaningful Message

If you must leave a message, here are a few pointers that ensure it will be taken and delivered correctly.

- Be brief. Use short, easy-to-write and -read sentences.
- Be organized. If there is more than a single, simple thought, you should organize it for the message taker.

> "I have three things to tell Claire. First. . . . Second. . . . Third . . ."

- Have it repeated. Ask the message taker to read it back so you can be sure that *you* were clear. Don't imply that the message taker could have gotten it wrong.
- Ask the name of the message taker. The reason you do this is psychological. People feel more committed to getting the message taken and delivered if they have some ownership or responsibility for it. However, asking for a name could also sound threatening or intimidating, which is the opposite of what you want. So, as soon as you give your message, thank that person for their help, then ask:

  You: "May I ask your name?"
  Message taker: "Erica."
  You: "Thank you for your help, Erica. I really appreciate it."

- Keep a record of your call. Jot down the date, time, message left, name of person who helped, and disposition of the call. Do this for each call. You'll be very glad when you need to remember the call.

Making calls presents you with a special opportunity to make a positive, professional impression. Use your judgment about how chatty to be when you call. It is nice to let people know that you're a friendly person, but don't get the reputation of being a real talker.

Taking Calls

It may or may not be your job to *take* calls at work, but everyone does it. Some calls will be easy, organized, direct, even friendly. Some will be difficult, disorganized, indirect, and unfriendly. Here are a few pointers for taking calls.

1. Prepare Your Company Greeting

Often, your greeting is prescribed by your company.

> "Good morning, Tobias Stationary."
> "Volak Fish Farm, may I help you?"

If you answer calls from outside your company, be good at it! Say the appropriate greeting clearly and slowly enough to be understood. When was the last time you called someplace and on the other end you heard "CLANJERSPASTESHOPSHO" (click). How frustrating! Anyone calling for the first time could be totally lost. How about getting this response when placing a long-distance call? You're not only confused but you're spending money! "Claire and Jerry's Pastry Shop. Please hold," is at least understandable. This takes practice. Say the name of your company frequently so you know what it should sound like. Some companies have names that are difficult to articulate or understand over the phone. Try saying your greeting five times fast. It takes practice. Don't be shy— practice your company name, maybe even your own name. One of our favorites is a business called Fred's Fun Box. They say "Box" when answering incoming calls.

2. Prepare Your Own Greeting

How do *you* answer the phone?

> "Yo."
> "What's happenin' "
> "Talk to me."
> "It's your dime."
> "Hello."
> "Howdy."
> "This is Lea, why are you calling me?"

You should decide how you wish to answer your phone. It says something about your attitude, mood, and willingness to talk or to be helpful. We repeat, a phone call is an opportunity, not an interruption. We know, the temptation is sometimes strong to pick up the receiver and shout, "What do you want?" Don't do it. Be polite, professional, and courteous.

3. The Hold Button Is Not a Weapon!

Don't use the hold button to explode an obnoxious, annoying, or irritating caller into the never-never land of hold. In fact, if you can avoid putting people on hold, that's even better. Do you like being put on hold? How long are you willing to wait? What does it feel like to be on hold? Most likely, very unpleasant and unproductive. No one likes to be kept waiting on hold. Many businesses try to soften the experience of being on hold. The most popular device has been music. Some companies tune into a local radio station. Have you called an airline or a movie theater lately? They play commercials for their products or services. One company uses Jokes on Hold. Great idea? Wrong. People would pick up the phone before the punch line and upset the holding caller. An intriguing idea was suggested by a well-meaning but overworked receptionist with as many as 10 lines on hold who said, "While you're waiting, would you care to speak with someone else who's on hold?"

There is a better way! When you put people on hold:

- Tell them that you're going to put them on hold.
- Tell them why.
- Estimate the time they'll be on hold.
- Offer them the option of calling back.
- Thank them before you place them on hold.

When you return to holding callers:

- Thank them for waiting.
- If the person they want to speak to still isn't available, and you have to put them on hold for a little while longer, say that you know how difficult it is to be on hold.

Callers understand that hold is important, and maybe inevitable. They really appreciate hearing that you're sensitive to their impatience and value their time.

Remember, putting people on hold is another opportunity to make a positive, professional impression.

4. Take Complete and Accurate Messages

When you take messages, you become a critical conduit of communication. Taking messages well is an extremely important skill. Your co-workers will appreciate a well-taken message. In fact, it can make or break a customer deal or soothe an upset client. When taking a message for someone else:

- Write it down as you get it. Don't depend on your memory.
- Repeat the message to the caller. This shows you were listening and will leave an accurate message.
- Get the name and phone number of the caller. Ask for correct spelling of all names, titles, and so on.

- In addition to correct spelling, write all names and unusual terms in *"fonetiks"*. This will help your co-workers pronounce the words correctly.
- Don't use jargon or abbreviations that may be misunderstood.
- Time, date, and sign the message.

5. Be Helpful

Try to help callers even if you are not the specific person who can help them, by connecting them to the person who can. To ensure your helpfulness, use the VIP technique.

V	Be *vocal*. Talk. Don't wait for the caller to do all the talking. Ask how you can be helpful.
I	Be *informative*. If you can't supply the exact information, help the caller find it.
P	Be *personable*, not *personal*. Use a pleasant tone and clear articulation, be polite when asking for information, be friendly when volunteering assistance, and use good, active listening skills.

6. Know Your System

Understand how your phone system works. Know how to put people on hold without cutting them off. Learn how to transfer calls or return the caller to the operator.

7. Screen Calls Appropriately

When screening calls, you take an incoming call and try to find out who is calling and what the caller wants. Screening is most commonly done by a receptionist who needs to direct calls, and by secretaries and assistants who need to protect their supervisors' time.

Screening calls can be tricky. Callers usually don't like to be screened. It feels like they are being evaluated or judged. Some callers go so far as to say that they don't like being evaluated or judged by someone who isn't qualified enough, smart enough, or important enough to appreciate the worthiness of the call. It is quite irritating to callers to be screened. If you must screen calls, be careful. Here a few pointers:

- Sound concerned about the caller's wishes.
- Ask for clarification to be certain that you understand the caller's wishes.
- Explain why the party who was called is not available.
- Volunteer to be helpful yourself.
- Take an accurate message.
- Thank the caller for patience and understanding and give assurance that the message will be delivered.
- Do what you said — deliver an accurate message.

Special Situations

In the following situations, you may need every one of the skills and techniques you've learned in this chapter. These are special opportunities to make a positive, professional impression.

Telephone Customer Service Skills

Telemarketing is selling on the phone. Telemarketing didn't even exist 25 years ago. The telephone companies created telemarketing and it has become an important industry. There are even companies that do telemarketing for other companies. More importantly, it's a tool used by many companies to serve their existing customers and to reach potential new customers. At some point, you may be expected to know what telemarketing is and how to do it.

You have probably been called by someone trying to interest you in anything from magazine subscriptions to time-sharing property to donations for special causes to surveys for a local radio station. We hate to remind you, but you've probably even been telemarketed by a computer call. Ugh! Telemarketing is a highly organized and increasingly mechanized business tool.

Some companies use telemarketing to sell investments. The caller shows up to work at 4:30 P.M. and receives a list of 200 telephone names and numbers that has been prepared that day. The list is made up of prospects that have been "prequalified"; that is, they have been researched and are likely investors, therefore worthy of being telemarketed. Between 5:00 and 8:00 P.M., the caller is expected to complete 200 calls. No, it's not impossible. It's a numbers game. Most of the calls take less than 30 seconds, then on to the next, and the next, and the next. How do telemarketers do it? They use a carefully crafted script, persistence, practice, and a tolerance for people hanging up on them. The following is a typical telemarketing script. Companies tailor a script like this to suit their own needs. Some telemarketing scripts are more aggressive than others. Some may not even sound like scripts. There are almost as many varieties of scripts as there are telemarketers.

Sample Telemarketing Script

Good evening, my name is _____ . I'm calling from _____ (name of company). We recently sent you a packet of information about our investment opportunities for the new season. Have you received the packet?

If YES, go to Box A   If NO, go to Box D

Box A

1. "Do you have an investment strategy?"
2. "Are you connected to an investment company to help implement this strategy?"
3. "Are you interested in hearing about *more* ways to invest and increase your income?"
   If YES, go to Box B
   If NO, go to Box C

Box B

1. Ask qualifying questions to determine if potential clients can make the minimum investment in your plan and follow investment procedures. (Your manager will provide qualifying guidelines.)

If clients qualify, go to Box C
If clients do *not* qualify, go to Box D

Box C

1. Ask qualified potential clients: "Would you like to hear more about opening an investment account with us?"

If YES, go to item 2 below
If NO, go to Box D

2. Set up a time to meet interested potential clients in person. Make sure the meeting time and place are convenient for the clients. Mark the meeting time and date on your schedule and call clients the day before to remind them of your appointment.

Box D

1. Determine potential clients' objections. Respond to these objections by listening to clients and using the information in your training packet under "Common Objections." (Get this material from your supervisor.)

If, after responding to clients' concerns, they still object, go to Box E item 2.

If client's objections are overcome, go to Box C item 2.

Box E

1. Tell clients what steps are needed to qualify and meet requirements in Box B Step 1 above.
2. If clients are still uninterested, terminate the call by thanking them for their patience and offer to be of assistance if they reconsider their position.

Box F

1. "Well, a packet of information about our investment opportunities will arrive in the mail shortly. I'll be in touch again soon to tell you more about our investment plans, and answer any questions you may have."
2. Give clients your name and phone number if they want to call you after receiving the investment information.
3. Apologize for interrupting clients' evening (or afternoon), thank them for their times, and say goodbye.

Telemarketing is such a prominent part of business, there are many books available on particular techniques. If it may be part of your work, we encourage you to find one of these books and dedicate time to developing your telemarketing skills Each company has its own purpose and style. Not everyone gives you a prequalified or long list, or pursues such an aggressive pattern for telemarketing. You will need to adjust to your particular company. Then, of course, all of the other skills you are learning in this text will be valuable.

Upset Callers

Upset callers can be very upsetting to you. They may shout, accuse, degrade, name call, threaten, or cry. Remember, don't take it personally! This is an opportunity, not an interruption. Here is a terrific technique for handling upset callers. These words are not set in stone—you may be creative. However, the order in which you say whatever you say is very important. The technique is called F-F-F.

> *First F:* "I understand how you *feel*." Be sure you don't say this until callers have said everything they want to say. Don't interrupt, even if you've heard the whole story before. If you do interrupt an upset caller, what will the caller say?
>
> "You don't understand; you won't even let me finish. You're not listening." So be patient.
>
> *Second F:* "I have *felt* the same way." Here, use a 10-second personal anecdote to indicate that you can identify with the caller's feelings.
>
> "I've felt the same way when I waited home all day for the telephone repair crew to show up. It wasted my whole day. I understand your feeling of frustration."
>
> Don't take longer than 10 seconds. An upset caller doesn't want to hear a long story from you.
>
> *Third F:* "I have *found* that what helps is. . . ."
> Then give a solution or plan for assistance.

This feel, felt, found technique works very well. Add your own words to it and practice saying it in a calm, patient, understanding tone.

Voice Mail

You may love it or hate it, but voice mail is here to stay. Voice mail is an automated answering service similar to the answering machine system you may use at home. "It's time-consuming." "It wastes time." "It's efficient." "It's cumbersome." It all depends on who you talk to. Everyone seems to agree that the worst part is getting put in "voice mail jail." You may have been there. Voice mail jail is when you are lost in a system that gives you options but none of them are what you need and there is no live human being at the other end. *If,* and it's a big if, you get to a place where you can at least leave a message, here are a few pointers.

1. Be brief. Keep your message as short as possible.
2. Be organized. Think about the message before you call and put your thoughts in order.
3. Be clear. Speak clearly and directly into your mouthpiece. Give special attention to names and numbers.
4. Be aware. Some people use voice mail and answering machines to screen calls. They may actually be listening to your message as you speak.

Developing a Good Phone Manner

Beyond specific telephone skills such as taking and making calls, using the hold button, using a telemarketing script, and handling upset callers, there are also general skills you can apply to all your business phone calls. Keep in mind that telephone calls are an excellent opportunity to promote your company's image and develop a good relationship and reputation with your clients, customers, and colleagues.

We all know people who have a wonderful phone manner. They are the colleagues at work who never seem ruffled by even the most problematic callers, never get confused or thrown off balance by out-of-the-ordinary calls, and never view phone calls as interruptions, to be avoided at all costs. We've analyzed these people's skills to determine what elements make up a good telephone manner. By mastering the following skills, you'll gain telephone confidence and add to your business speaking skills.

1. Keep a positive attitude.
2. Live the golden rule: Do unto others as you would have them do unto you.
3. Never lose your temper.
4. Be a good listener. Everyone likes to be listened to.
5. Treat others with respect. *Everyone* gets special treatment.
6. Always speak politely and courteously.
7. Have patience and tolerance with the shortcomings of others.
8. Understand human behavior, especially human needs.
9. Practice stress management regularly. Do whatever works for you, but do something.
10. Use the F-F-F technique frequently.
11. Separate personal and professional attitudes and behaviors.
12. Sound appropriately concerned about people's needs.
13. Smile with your face and your voice.
14. Take messages well.
15. Use the hold button courteously.
16. Maintain a neat, professional appearance at all times. This helps maintain a positive attitude that can be heard over the phone.
17. Provide options when problem solving. Be open to the ideas of others.
18. Offer to help in any situation.
19. Develop alternate methods for ending a call. Remember—it's an opportunity, not an interruption.
20. Use people's last names with their titles frequently (Mrs. or Dr. Nikolof, not Ann). Be respectful, but not too chummy.

Naturally, these elements and characteristics must be developed within your personal style. For instance, some people don't use humor as a means of relating to people. But you might have a natural tendency and talent for using humor on the phone. Humor is a great tool for enhancing communication. If you can use humor well, you'll be able to handle many tricky phone situations. Remember, this list of skills should be personalized and adapted to your needs. Be creative and express your individuality on the phone. Become an expert at telephone problem solving and trouble shooting. After all, telephone communication is here to stay—be an effective master of this business tool and enhance your business speaking skills.

Chapter Review

- The telephone is a business machine—be ready to use it for *business*.
- The telephone is an opportunity, not an interruption.
- Never speak longer than one minute without allowing the person on the other end of the phone to react.
- Practice active listening while on the phone.
- When making calls, prepare ahead with a plan for the call.
- When making calls, always ask if it is a convenient time to talk.
- When leaving a message, be succinct, ask the name of the message taker, and thank him or her by name.
- Use the VIP technique to give a positive, helpful, professional impression.
- The hold button is not a weapon. Practice putting people on and taking them off hold.
- When taking messages, be thorough and include the time and date of the message.
- Telemarketing is here to stay. Learn how your company does it and practice that technique.

Practice Exercises

1. While sitting back-to-back with a classmate, practice making and taking two separate calls. Emphasize greeting, message giving, and message taking.
2. In small groups of four or five, practice the F-F-F technique. Give feedback on the technique and on the listening skills utilized.

3. Call two local department stores and ask for information regarding the price and availability of a particular item. Report to the class on the similarities and differences of these calls.

4. Devise your individual version of phone manner. Divide into small groups of four or five and practice your version with other group members role-playing various types of callers. Then, get feedback and try it again.

Quick Quiz

1. As a business machine, the telephone is an opportunity, not an
   _____ .

2. What business machine is frequently found in the home?

3. When you are on the phone, you represent your company's
   _____ .

4. What should be the maximum time length of personal calls conducted at work?

5. Why is eating while on the phone a bad idea?

6. How long should you speak before allowing the person on the other end of the phone to participate?

7. What does having a plan before making a call mean?

8. To avoid being a slavemaster as a caller, what should you ask?

9. How can you ensure that the message you leave will be delivered accurately?

10. What is "voice mail jail"?

11 Using Visual Aids

"Effective communication can make the difference between the success or failure of a business executive. Communication takes many forms—it goes beyond standard oral and written presentation. Of critical importance to one's success is personal presentation. In business, we are often judged by a first impression: The way we look, the way we speak, the way we shake hands. That first impression may serve as an everlasting impression, so make it your best."
Lesley Berkovitz, *Vice President, Human Resources, Sunglass Hut*

Chapter Objectives

After reading this chapter you will be able to:

1. Understand the most common purposes of visual aids in business speaking: clarification and emphasis.
2. Use a variety of visual aids.
3. Create an effective overhead transparency.
4. Synchronize your use of visual aids with a presentation or speech.

This chapter will teach you how to effectively use visual aids during business speaking. The tremendous boom in technology available to business professionals has even produced an expectation that speakers will use visuals as part of business presentations. If you *don't* use visual aids, your presentation could appear incomplete.

Most business presentations and meetings use overhead transparencies, so we will focus on those. However, we will also discuss the other popular media such as slides, flip charts, and video. In addition, we will look at the growing utilization of computer-generated visuals.

Our more specific objectives include introducing techniques for using any type of visual; differentiating when to use which type of visual aid; and suggestions for room layout.

What Are Visual Aids?

Visual aids are materials you can use to help your listeners understand, accept, and be motivated by your speaking. The most common visual aids are:

- Flip charts.
- Overhead transparencies.
- Slides.
- Film.
- Video.
- Scale models.
- Charts and graphs.

Many businesses have visual aids that are useful to their line of work, products, or services. There is, however, one visual aid that is the same in every business presentation. You—the speaker—are also a visual aid. Listeners judge your information and ideas partly by the way you look. The speaker as a visual aid is so important that we talk about it separately in Chapter 8, Nonverbal Communication.

It is also important to recognize that the speaker is not a *human aid*— that is, not an aid to the visual. The visual is there to aid the speaker! You are the expert. It is your opportunity to shine. Don't let the visuals or the technology be more interesting, attractive, or valuable than what you bring to the situation.

Why Use Visuals?

There are two common purposes for using visuals. The first is *clarification*. If you are concerned that information or an idea may not be clear or easy for listeners to understand or follow, use a visual. The second purpose is *emphasis*. If you want to stress that information or an idea is *very important* to the listener, use a visual aid. In addition, it is often helpful to use a visual for dramatic effect, for visual variety, or for a visual break in a long presentation.

Whatever else you do, don't hide behind your visuals. Sometimes, speakers who are nervous use visuals as a way of distracting attention from themselves. Position the visuals slightly off center in the room to allow the speaker center stage. Learn to control your nervousness. You already know some control techniques from mastering the Silver Square from Chapter 2. Don't misuse visuals to mask your nervousness.

Also, do not use visuals as speaker notes. We know that it is very easy for you to prompt your thinking by looking at the information and ideas on the visual. However, it is harmful to your credibility and control to allow listeners to read your thoughts before you have the opportunity to introduce them. Visuals should reinforce your ideas, not be a substitute for them.

Types of Visuals

There are many types of visuals used in business speaking, some of which we listed earlier in this chapter. Here is a brief description of the most commonly used visual aids.

Flip Chart

A flip chart is a large pad of paper attached to an easel or stand of some kind. Flip charts are very common and are often a normal part of conference rooms. Occasionally, you will find them in a wall-mounted unit containing white boards and felt boards. They are popular because they are easy to use, portable, and inexpensive. Although prices vary somewhat, they average $10 per pad. They are effective for groups up to about 30 listeners.

Flip charts are best used for interactive speaking. They are effective for creating the visual as you speak and for helping your listeners focus on it. Many speakers like to create the flip chart visual, then tear it off and tape it up on the wall as a reminder while they create the next one. Make sure the pad is securely attached to its stand so it won't flip onto you! This allows you to write on all parts of the paper without fear of the stand or pad flipping over. Some stands are really only triangular easels designed to display signs. These do not provide support for the upper corners of the flip chart. As a result, you will have an impossible time writing on the pad. This, of course, can hurt your overall effectiveness as a speaker. Use a magic marker or heavy pen on flip charts, not an ordinary pen or pencil. Remember to always check that your marker is moist and full, not dried up.

Flip Chart

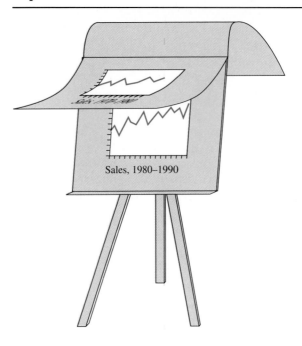

Sales, 1980–1990

Overhead Transparencies

An overhead transparency is an 8½-by 11-inch piece of acetate or clear plastic that can be written or typed on. Transparencies are placed on an overhead projector, which focuses the image onto a screen on the wall. They may be clear or in colors. They are purchased in boxes of 50 to 100 pieces. You buy the blank transparencies and write or type your words and images on the acetate. You've probably seen these used in the classroom or at work. They are variously referred to as *overheads, transparencies, acetates,* or *foils*. They are effective for almost any size group since the screen and projection size can be controlled. They are most commonly used with groups of 30 or more people. The projector can cost as little as $200 or as much as $1,200, depending on the features. Most business centers, conference facilities, and hotels supply projectors as standard audiovisual equipment.

The transparencies themselves can be used just like a flip chart or piece of paper. It is also possible to produce transparencies that look exactly like slides and photographs. (We'll discuss this more when we cover computer-generated visual aids.) Naturally, the cost will vary. More elaborately produced transparencies can cost $75 or more. The most effective use of transparencies is to focus listeners and allow for interaction. You can face your listeners as you use the transparencies, changing from transparency to transparency quickly and easily.

Be aware that there are a few pitfalls to using transparencies. They are so easy to use that many speakers *overuse* them. They use too many, and put too much data on each one. As with all visuals, the ideal is *one thought* equals *one visual*. Speakers often abuse this guideline and put many thoughts or topics on one. In fact, there is a terrible technique that we see all too often called *rip and read*. A speaker will literally rip a page from a book or report, transfer it to a transparency by running it through the office copy machine, then read it to the listeners. Boring! Insulting! Ineffective!

Always try to put your transparencies in a frame. Frames are designed to give your transparencies a neat and uniform appearance. Plus, they prevent the otherwise flimsy piece of acetate from slip-sliding right off the projector.

When you use transparencies, don't turn the light on and off, on and off each time you change transparencies. It is cumbersome for you as the speaker and visually annoying and distracting to your listeners. The only people who benefit are those who make the light bulbs. Speaking of light bulbs, be sure to check that the light bulb is working before you use the projector. Whenever possible, have a spare bulb handy, just in case. Some projectors even come equipped with a spare bulb built into the machine.

We will give a few more pointers about the content of transparencies a bit later in this chapter when we focus on designing visuals.

Transparency Graph

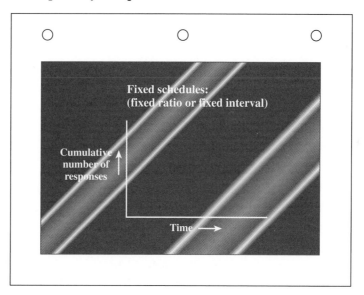

Slides

Slides are photographs that have been put on 35 mm film. Slides are the preferred medium for bigger crowds, repeated presentations, and whenever you want to give a more professional look to your presentation. Slides are an investment, as they can be expensive to produce. Here is a typical comparison of the same design and information.

Transparency	*Slide*
Words only: $5 Words and artwork: $20	Words only: $30 Words and artwork: $90

Slides require a projector to focus the image on a screen or the wall. The projector can cost as little as $200 or as much as $1,200, depending on the features. Of course, the major difference between slides and almost any other visual aid is that you must turn the lights out to use them. You can just dim the lights, but the darker the room, the sharper and clearer your slides will look.

Be aware that putting your listeners in the dark can take the shine out of your speaking. Don't use slides to hide in the dark. This is a worn-out trick used by ineffective speakers. Turn the lights out only as long as needed.

The slide projector also depends on a light bulb. Be sure it works, and carry a spare just in case. For smaller groups of three to five people, you may find it more effective to use a self-contained slide projector that has the screen built in. These look like small microwave ovens and are convenient for tabletop presentation.

Video

Video is TV. It is the same technology that is used to produce network programs — on a smaller scale, of course. For use in business speaking, you will need a preproduced videotape, a VCR to play the tape, and a TV set to view the tape. You may want to use a larger screen projector for bigger groups. A cost-effective use of video is for employee training. Producing videos for monthly meetings, changing progress reports, or staff meetings is usually not practical.

We can't treat video too lightly, however. Outside the business world, in society at large, video has become the most popular toy or tool of almost every family. It is indeed a familiar technology and form of communication.

Be aware, however, that what is tolerated, even expected, of home videos is by no means acceptable in business videos. Poorly produced video can destroy an otherwise effective business presentation. When it isn't home video, people expect Hollywood. Of course, you can go overboard, too. Video that is too slick can dominate you as the speaker. The effective use of video in business speaking is much more than standing a few folks in front of your handycam and superimposing a title and date. If you do have a well-produced videotape, be sure that you have the appropriate equipment to match your tape. Unlike transparencies and slides, where it's basically ''one size fits all,'' videotapes and their accompanying machines come in many sizes. This is not a technical textbook on videotape, so we won't go into detail on the differences. The most commonly used size is ½-inch VHS, but before you use it, check it out.

Film

Film is more scarce every year. It is expensive to produce and cumbersome to use. There are many fine preproduced films on the market, but even these are being transferred to videotape. With the exception of training classes, the use of film as an aid to business speaking is nearly nonexistent.

If you do use film, you (or someone) need to know how to thread the projector and how to splice the film back together if it breaks during your presentation. Remember, you'll be doing all this in the dark, since the lights must be turned out when using film. And don't forget the light bulb.

Scale Models

Scale models are three-dimensional products. We don't see models used frequently. They can be expensive to produce and have little value in most business speaking. Architecture is an obvious example of a business that could logically utilize models.

Models can be so interesting to look at that they can easily distract attention from the speaker. If you do use a model, employ the three guidelines for using visuals, discussed later in this chapter. They will help both you and your listeners.

Charts and Graphs

Charts and graphs are used often but can be confusing. Speakers often believe that a chart is a chart is a chart and a graph is a graph is a graph. Not true. Some are more effective than others in depicting certain types of data. Experiment with the different formats to determine which type of chart presents your information in the clearest, most effective way.

Here are some examples:

Percentage of annual salary used for various expenses

Savings 12%
Food 25%
Travel 13%
Tuition 10%
Rent 40%

Pie Chart

Bar Chart

Line Graph

Computer Graphics

In the entertainment and advertising fields, computer-generated graphics are used more and more frequently and to great effect. Next time you watch the news, look at the graphics of expanding and deflating dollar bills or self-building pie charts formed behind the newscaster— these were created using computer-generated graphics. High-technology visual aids are also used creatively in advertising and in television commercials. You may have seen ads when a man's head turns into a stylized square in a shaving commercial, a car turns into a tiger, or a mailman turns into a high-flying eagle. In the movies, alien creatures emerge from human bodies, police officers turn into silver and chrome androids, and singers in music videos change form and shape in time to their music. This computer-driven transformation process is called *morphing*.

Some businesses use this type of complex computer-generated graphic to make visual aids in business presentations. For instance, a telephone software company could use a morphing graphic to show information received by their product, broken down into millions of information particles, reformed, and correctly chanelled through a communication system. This would certainly make an effective video contribution to a large sales presentation. However, this use of computer-generated graphics is very expensive and time-consuming in a business setting. Incorporating computer-generated graphics, and then learning to synchronize them with spoken text, requires complicated software and hardware and usually special training. Often, business speakers don't have the time or money to use computer-generated graphics in their video format as seen on television or described in the example above.

However, it *is* increasingly common to generate static images on a computer and translate these into overhead slides and transparencies. This type of "flat" graphic can be created through very sophisticated processes, or through more accessible means. For our purposes here, we'll discuss "flat" computer graphics you can make with common computer systems. Because many computer programs offer interesting typefaces, the ability to draw on screen, and all types of format and design options, speakers can create lively, interesting pieces to be used as transparencies. It's a good idea to familiarize yourself with the software options on your school's shared computer system, if there is one. Many companies have a *mainframe* computer with designing and graphic features that everyone can access. Some companies have personal computers (PCs) with a wide variety of design features to use to create slides or transparencies. After you've designed the transparency or slide (remember, only one concept per transparency), print it out and bring it to a service that translates your paper image into a transparency or slide format. Large companies may have this service done by an in-house visual aids department. If your company doesn't have the ability to create transparencies, look in a telephone book under graphics, arts, copying, and slides.

Both of the following graphics were created on personal computers.

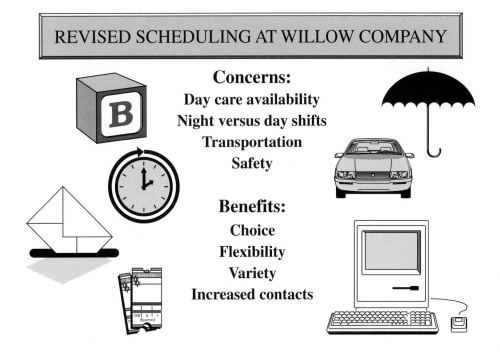

Over the past two years we've conducted a survey of speaking practices and preferences among more than 1,000 business speakers throughout the United States. The survey produced the following interesting data on the most commonly used visual aids.

Overhead transparencies are used 44 percent of the time.

Slides are used 30 percent of the time.

Flip charts are used 12 percent of the time.

Videos are used 8 percent of the time.

Models are used 4 percent of the time.

Others are used 2 percent of the time.

As you can see, overhead transparencies and slides are clearly the most commonly used visuals. Because they are so popular, here are a few pointers about the design and preparation of these visuals.

Overhead Transparencies

- One thought per overhead.
- No more than 12 words per overhead.
- Don't use the rip and read technique (ripping a page out of a report, copying it onto an overhead, then reading it to listeners).
- Use a simple typeface such as Helvetica.
- Use colored acetate transparencies for interest and emphasis.
- Use bold, black print.
- When you use darker acetate like green or dark blue, use a lighter color print such as yellow or pink.
- Use cardboard frames around acetate transparencies.
- Number each overhead on a corner of the frame.
- Use graphics such as symbols and characters only if you're sure the listeners will not think they are silly.
- Graphics should add structure, emphasis, or organization—not decoration.
- Don't write sideways on graphics or charts.

Slides

- One thought per slide.
- No more than 12 words per slide.
- Slide projectors easily distort print, so space your print slightly further apart than usual to allow for blurring.
- Simple type works well in slides as well as transparencies.
- Avoid type with serifs (lines projecting from the main body of the letter), which may blur when viewed with the projector.

- Reading slides is like reading the print on a lit light bulb, so use a dark background with lighter print colors.
- Don't write sideways on graphs and charts.

Naturally, you must judge the design and preparation of your slides and overheads according to the needs of each speaking situation.

Visuals Worksheet

The worksheet on the next page will help you organize and integrate your visuals into your speech.

Simply draw a rough sketch of your visual in the box on the right-hand side of the worksheet. In the Notes column to the left of the box, put whatever ideas you wish to convey while the visual is being viewed by your listeners. The worksheet will also help you feel comfortably in control of your presentation by showing what is coming up next. Try it.

Guidelines for Using Visuals

Here are the three most important guidelines you will need for using visuals. These apply to using *any* visual format or technology.

1. Synchronization

When you speak, you are communicating information over two channels—audio and video—at the same time. You must keep these two channels *synchronized*. Be sure that the visual aid you are using supports and matches what you are saying. Conversely, be sure you use a visual at the same time you are speaking about it. Show the visual to your listeners *only* during the time you are actually talking about that topic. It is very easy for listeners to get out of sync, confused, and even angry if your audio and video channels are not in sync. You know how you feel when the sound and the picture don't match when you are in a movie theater. Moviegoers may show their displeasure by shouting and stomping their feet until synchronization is restored. Business listeners won't be that demonstrative, but they may do one or all of the following:

- Stare at you.
- Glare at you.
- Squint at you.
- Take a nap.
- Talk to a neighbor.
- Get angry.
- Ask challenging questions.
- Ask pointless questions.
- Tune out.
- Leave.

Avoid these reactions by keeping your audio and video messages in sync.

Visuals Worksheet

Notes	*Visuals*

2. Introduction and Setup

Using the techniques of introduction and setup will help you keep your listeners in sync.

Introduction means that you should introduce every visual to listeners before you show it to them. Yes, we heard that gasp of astonishment! Most business speakers don't think it's necessary to introduce every visual. They would rather use their visuals as cue cards. They like to put the overhead or the slide on the screen, look it over, allowing the visual to prompt their remarks. This is easier than using notes. The important question is, "Easier on whom?" Certainly, it's easier for the speaker. However, these speakers are off target. Their efforts should be directed at making things easier for the listener, not the speaker! Introduce every visual! The introduction need only be a word or two, such as:

> "Here is a pie chart that. . ."
> "This next bar graph shows. . ."
> "Now, I'll review a list of cities where. . ."

Even these simple introductions spoken before the visual is seen will help your listeners "sync up" or get prepared to see a graph, chart, list, or whatever. Sometimes, it is necessary to use a bit more introduction. For instance:

> "The line graph I'm about to show you measures the investment potential by two factors. The left axis indicates market growth and the bottom axis indicates time."
> "This pie chart depicts the various product lines and their sales volume by color. The lighter colors indicate the weaker producers and the darker colors indicate the stronger producers."

If you don't use an introduction, whether simple or detailed, and merely show the visual, your listeners will be forced to tune out temporarily while they figure out what the data means. Help yourself. Help your listener. Introduce every visual.

Setup is slightly different than introduction. Setup means that you draw particular attention to a specific part of the visual you are introducing. Setup is used when the visual contains more information than you need or will be covering and you can't reduce or remove the extraneous data. You help yourself and your listener when you set up the visual. For example:

> "On this next diagram, please direct your attention to the area circled in red."
> "This blueprint of the basement is complex. To help us stay together as we move through the space, look at the yellow arrow in the lower left of the visual."

Your listeners will gladly follow your directions if it helps them understand a busy visual. Make a judgment to use *setup* if you have any doubt about listeners' familiarity with the data on the visual. Don't be shy about setup! Business listeners appreciate it and it sets you up as an authoritative, confident speaker.

3. Talk and Do

Talking and doing at the same time is a physical skill. It may sound silly but some speakers can't talk and do something else at the same time, such as change an overhead, write on a flip chart, or hand out materials. Listeners shouldn't have to sit and wait while you do housekeeping chores like these. Business listeners are usually busy, often preoccupied people. They appreciate it when speakers are organized, coordinated, and prepared to handle the functional tasks accompanying business speaking. You must practice the physical movements that may be required during your speaking. You will look and feel more comfortable, credible, and in control.

Your Setting

One often-forgotten aspect of using visuals is room layout. In fact, many speakers don't even think about it, or they believe that they must work with whatever is set up when they get to the room. There may be times when you must work with whatever you are given, but don't be afraid to move the furniture. The following is a diagram of two effective room setups for using slides and overheads. Notice how these setups also keep the speaker directly in front of the audience.

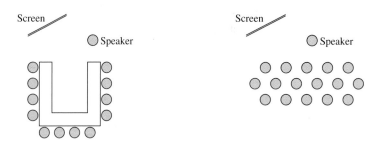

Chapter Review

- Visuals should be used during business speaking for two reasons:
  1. Clarification of information.
  2. Emphasis of information.
- Visual aids get their name because they aid the speaker. The speaker should not be a human aid for the visuals.
- Keep your visuals simple and easy to read. Keep them brief.
- Use one thought per visual.
- Overhead transparencies and slides are the most commonly used visuals in business speaking.
- When using visuals, remember to:

  Keep them synchronized with what you are saying.
  Introduce each visual to help prepare the listener for what is coming.
  Set up the more complicated visuals by drawing listeners' attention to a specific part of the visual just before you show it.
  Talk and do while you use visuals; don't allow gaps of silence while listeners watch you play with your visuals.

- Position the visuals slightly off center in the room to allow the speaker center stage.

Practice Exercises

The best way to practice using visuals is with a partner who can give you feedback. A video camera can also be very helpful. Yes, you will know if it "feels" right as you do it, but it is also very valuable to have another view (literally) of your actions.

1. Present a 60-second speech using one main point. Use one visual to emphasize the theme.
2. Present a three-minute speech that has one main point. Use three visuals: the first to clarify your point, and the other two to emphasize your point. Be especially aware of using the introduction and setup techniques.
3. Present a five-minute speech that has two major points. Use at least four visuals to clarify and emphasize your point. Use the visuals worksheet to guide your organization and help control synchronization, introduction and setup, and talk and do.

4. Go to a library and check out its visual resources. Determine if your library is a good source for videos, charts, and films.

5. With a partner, pick a passage from your textbook and plan what kinds of physical actions you might use to highlight portions of the text. Then practice the talk and do technique to coordinate smooth action with text reading.

Quick Quiz

1. What are three visual aids commonly used with business speaking?

2. What are the two common purposes for using visuals?

3. What are the most important guidelines for using visuals in business speaking?

4. What does synchronization mean?

5. When should the introduction technique be used with visuals?

6. Is the talk and do technique a planning or physical skill?

7. When using transparencies, should the light be turned off between each transparency?

8. In business speaking, what is the difference between TV and video?

9. When making an overhead transparency, why is it important to show only one thought or idea per transparency?

10. Define *synchronization* as it relates to business speaking. Why is it important?

Sample Scripts and Practice Sheets

In this appendix, we provide practice sheets with extra exercises to hone two important business-speaking skills—making a good verbal impression in a job interview, and handling phone communications smoothly and effectively. These two business-speaking situations are faced by most people at many points over the course of a career and even within a single day on the job. In fact, these two skills are crucial to job success. Mastering the first skill is necessary to win the job you want. Practicing and refining the second skill will ensure daily job success and advancement.

Interviewing Skills

The interview is, of course, one type of meeting. Refer back to Chapter 6, Participating in Meetings, to review the self-sell technique. The basic tenets of this technique are:

1. Make a can-do statement.
2. Make a benefit statement.
3. Offer your qualifications for the job.
4. Describe your work style clearly.
5. Suggest post-interview action.

Although these guidelines will serve you in any type of interview, how do you incorporate them into a conversation between you and the interviewer? Above all, be aware that the interview is your chance to promote your strengths *throughout* the interview, not just when you're specifically asked about your qualifications. As shown below, your goal in the interview is to turn every question into an opportunity to promote your strengths. This is a skill that can be consciously practiced and perfected over many interviews. We suggest that you practice in informational interviews, while role-playing with classmates or friends, even by ''interviewing'' yourself on a tape recorder. The main objective is to be comfortable with the interview situation and to be prepared for the unexpected.

In the following interview scenarios, pay close attention to Exhibits A and B, as they will serve as models for completing Exhibit C. In the interviews in Exhibits A and B, Charles Martineau is applying for an entry-level customer service job for a chain of discount clothing stores called MARKRIGHT. Charles recently completed a course in business communication at the Southtown Business College. His interviewer is Karen Clarkson, from MARKRIGHT's personnel department. Charles has already sent a résumé and letter of inquiry to the personnel department in response to an advertisement in the *Southtown Sentinel*. Exhibit A provides a model of what *not* to say in an interview, while Exhibit B shows some possible responses to help Charles get the job. In Exhibit C, it's your turn to answer the interviewer, and in Exhibit D, you play the interviewer and ask a classmate to sell his or her qualifications to you.

Exhibit A: Interview Strategies to Avoid

Karen Clarkson: "So, Charles, tell me a little bit about your interest in this customer service job. I see from your résumé that you took most of your course work in business communications, but you also took quite a few classes in the computer science department."

Charles Martineau: "Yeah, I guess I look a little scattered in my interests don't I? I'm not that good at making up my mind, as you can tell. That's kind of why I'm here, too—I figured, why not give it a shot? What's there to lose? I guess I'm just the kind of guy who lets things happen. Hey, if it's right, it's meant to be; if not, then no harm done, I say."

KC: "Do you have any background in customer service? What do *you* think are the skills a good customer service representative needs?"

CM: "Ummm, well, I don't have any *specific* customer service experience—maybe I'm not really qualified? Wait, I worked in the school cafeteria for one semester and I worked at a supermarket— maybe that would count. I guess good customer service people need to know how to satisfy the customer. Beyond that, I'd have a tough time defining the job—it's what you make of it, I suppose."

KC: "What are some of your best qualities and strengths? What can you bring to MARKRIGHT?"

CM: "Well, a couple of things come to mind right off the bat. First of all, I'm quite bossy, according to my friends, and I can be very good at forcing other people to follow my orders. Also, I have a sense of humor and really enjoy joking and teasing with my friends. Some people think of me as the real "life of the party" type, so I bet I'd liven up any work group."

KC: "With those strengths in mind, tell me a little about what you perceive as your weaknesses as they may relate to job performance here at MARKRIGHT."

CM: "I guess my main weakness, and I hate to admit this, but I really can't get out of bed much before 8:00. I think I'd have an awfully hard time getting here by 8:30 every day. You know, I'm just not a morning person. Too bad you don't have any afternoon shifts; that's my best time really. I guess I could adapt—go out and get one of those siren alarm clocks!"

KC: "Well, that may be a problem, but let's move on. Where do you see yourself in five years?"

CM: "It's a toss-up really. On the one hand, I want to be the president of a large conglomerate. I can clearly see myself set up in a large office managing a group of employees, or maybe making long-range plans concerning research and development. But then, I also have the option of moving to the West. You see, my brother-in-law has a large ranch out there and has practically begged me to come out and help him. I guess this answer goes back to the first question you asked me—I don't know *what* will happen—I thrive on the challenge of the unexpected."

KC: "I see . . . well, I think our time is up now, Charles. Do you have any questions or comments for me?"

CM: "I guess not. See you around, then, goodbye."

Exhibit B: Interview Strategies to Get the Job and Sell Yourself

Karen Clarkson: "So, Charles, tell me a little bit about your interest in this customer service job. I see from your résumé that you took most of your course work in business communications, but you also took quite a few classes in the computer science department."

Charles Martineau: "Well, as you can see, I have a lot of interests. At the college, I had an idea to combine communication skills with high-tech skills since this looks to be the wave of the future in a lot of industries. This is particularly appropriate for customer service since I know MARKRIGHT reps are on-line with the inventory and distribution departments. Plus, I'm a natural communicator—I've always dealt well with people and I'm not easily ruffled. Customer service seems to me like a great place to put my varied skills to work! It's where the action is at a growing company like MARKRIGHT."

KC: "Do you have any background in customer service? What do *you* think are the skills a good customer service representative needs?"

CM: "Well, I've never held a job with the specific title 'Customer Service Rep,' but I've had a lot of experience dealing with the public as a cashier at Big Y Grocery. There I had to soothe a lot of angry or confused customers. I became quite skilled at anticipating problems before they arose, giving people direction to find the products and services they were looking for, and using all the assets of the store to help the customers even if I couldn't help them personally. I'd say that a good customer service rep knows how to think on his or her feet, can solve problems efficiently, can remain calm in a crisis, and knows how to use resources. I'd certainly say that *I* have those skills—I wouldn't have survived at Big Y without them!"

KC: "What are some of your best qualities and strengths? What can you bring to MARKRIGHT?"

CM: "I'm a real go-getter when it comes to finding solutions to tough problems. I have one of those bulldog mentalities when faced with a task that others claim is impossible. I guess I get this from my mother. She always told us kids that it takes elbow grease and hard work to get the big jobs done. I consider it a challenge to tackle problems and push myself. Believe me, this strength has been very handy in all my jobs, as well as at home and in school."

KC: "With those strengths in mind, tell me a little about what you perceive as your weaknesses as they may relate to job performance here at MARKRIGHT."

CM: "Well, sometimes I think I'm *too much* of a perfectionist. It's awfully hard for me to walk away from a problem or leave an assignment unfinished. Sometimes this bothers my wife, but I have to tell her that's just the way I am. So far this hasn't been a problem on the job, but it sure bugs my wife! She'll just have to blame my mother, I guess."

KC: "Well, I doubt that would be a problem here, but let's move on. Where do you see yourself in five years?"

CM: "I want to be on a learning and growth track here at MARKRIGHT. Since you're a growing company, it looks like there's a lot of room for moving between departments and exploring different areas. One goal is to help people work together as part of a productive team. For instance, I believe I could develop team strategies for the customer service and sales department to work together and increase overall business here at MARKRIGHT. I've had team experience at my last job and learned a lot there about group dynamics."

KC: "I see . . . well, I think our time is up now, Charles. Do you have any questions or comments for me?"

CM: "Well, I don't have any specific questions right now—we've covered a lot of ground and answered all my questions so far. I really think that I would fit in well here at MARKRIGHT, based on your requirements and my interests and qualifications. What I'd like to do now is call you in a few days to see what the next step is. As I said before, I feel good about MARKRIGHT and confident that I would be an asset to the company. Thanks for your time, and I'll talk to you very soon.''

Exhibit C: Sell Yourself

Fill in the blanks with your own responses to these common interview questions. Keep in mind that your goal is to show how your unique skills and qualifications make a perfect fit with the company's needs.

Karen Clarkson: ''So, tell me a little bit about your interest in this customer service job. I see from your résumé that you took most of your course work in business communications, but you also took quite a few classes in the computer science department.''

YOU: _____

_____

_____

_____

_____

KC: ''Do you have any background in customer service? What do *you* think are the skills a good customer service representative needs?''

YOU: _____

_____

_____

_____

_____

KC: ''What are some of your best qualities and strengths? What can you bring to MARKRIGHT?''

YOU: _____

_____

_____

_____

_____

KC: "With those strengths in mind, tell me a little about what you perceive as your weaknesses as they may relate to job performance here at MARKRIGHT."

YOU: _____

_____

_____

_____

_____

_____

KC: "Well, that's probably not a problem, but let's move on. Where do you see yourself in five years?"

YOU: _____

_____

_____

_____

_____

_____

KC: "I see . . . well, I think our time is up now. Do you have any questions or comments for me?"

YOU: _____

_____

_____

_____

_____

_____

Exhibit D: You're the Interviewer

Work with a partner and take turns playing the interviewer and the interviewee. Encourage the interviewee to bring up strengths at all possible opportunities.

INTERVIEWER: "So, tell me a little bit about your interest in this customer service job. I see from your résumé that you took most of your course work in business communications, but you also took quite a few classes in the computer science department."

INTERVIEWEE: _____

_____

_____

_____

_____

_____

INTERVIEWER: ''Do you have any background in customer service? What do *you* think are the skills a good customer service representative needs?''

INTERVIEWEE: _____

_____

_____

_____

_____

_____

INTERVIEWER: ''What are some of your best qualities and strengths? What can you bring to MARKRIGHT?''

INTERVIEWEE: _____

_____

_____

_____

_____

_____

INTERVIEWER: ''With those strengths in mind, tell me a little about what you perceive as your weaknesses as they may relate to job performance here at MARKRIGHT.''

INTERVIEWEE: _____

_____

_____

_____

_____

INTERVIEWER: ''Well, that's probably not a problem, but let's move on. Where do you see yourself in five years?''

INTERVIEWEE: _____

_____

_____

_____

_____

_____

INTERVIEWER: ''I see . . . well, I think our time is up now. Do you have any questions or comments for me?''

INTERVIEWEE: _____

_____

_____

_____

_____

_____

Sharpening Your Telephone Skills

Telephone communication skills are an important asset for any employee, from entry level all the way to the top. In Chapter 10, Effective Telephone Skills, we cover the basic skills everyone needs to turn business phone calls from interruptions to opportunities to promote your company's professional image. Refer back to Chapter 10 to refresh yourself on these basic guidelines for handling almost every routine call. But what happens when you get a phone call that is out of the ordinary? We've all heard the saying, ''The customer is always right,'' but sometimes this just doesn't go far enough. Suppose you run up against a caller who is angry and hostile, demanding, or simply won't get off the line? In Exhibits E, F, and G, we'll show you negative and positive reactions to this type of caller, and leave room for your response. When it's your turn to respond, use your creativity and imagination to handle the problem calls in your own way. Put your listening and communication skills to the test!

Exhibit E: Handling Angry Callers

The most important guideline to use when handling an angry customer, client, or colleague is to be sympathetic to the caller's perceived problem. Remember, even if *you* don't think the problem is valid or real, the person on the other end thinks it is very real indeed, and will not appreciate your making light of the situation. Put yourself in the caller's place and show respect at all times.

1. Give the caller time to vent steam. Let the caller finish speaking—don't interrupt. This shows you respect the caller's right to a thoughtful and helpful answer. At this point, you're there to listen to the caller's *valid* complaint.

Angry caller: "I can't believe I still haven't received the sweater I ordered from MARKRIGHT!!! It says right in your catalog that you deliver items within two working days. I am so sick of false claims that trick people out of their hard-earned cash. I promised my daughter the sweater she wanted, and now have *nothing* to give her! What's going on here—do I have to report you to the Better Business Bureau to get any satisfaction?!"

Unhelpful response: "Calm down, lady, I can't believe you're getting all worked up over nothing. I just work here, so lay off, OK? I'm *not* paid to sit here and take this!!!"

Helpful response: "Well, it sounds like you have reason to feel irritated. It must have been tough to disappoint your daughter. I sure know how bad it can feel when you can't follow through on a promise, especially when it's no fault of your own."

Your helpful response: _____

_____

_____

_____

_____

_____

2. Offer possible explanations for the customer's problem. Apologize for inconveniencing the customer. This tells the customer that you recognize his or her discomfort. This validates the customer's right to get satisfaction.

Angry caller: "So, can you tell me how this happened? I mean it says right here, 'Two-Day Delivery Guaranteed.' Am I supposed to believe this or not?"

Unhelpful response: "Look, what's the big deal? Life has its little ups and downs and it's no use getting so worked up over nothing! You really need to get some perspective."

Helpful response: "I *am* sorry that you've been put out this way. Maybe it has something to do with a glitch in the warehouse, or maybe we mistyped your ZIP code. Sometimes, we get a big rush order and our stockroom runs out of popular items. Let me see what I can do."

Your helpful response: _____

_____

_____

_____

_____

3. Solve the problem immediately, if possible. Remember, most employees have been hired to be problem solvers. Look at this call as an opportunity to crack a tough problem case. Offer solutions that will help calm the customer and show that you value his or her continued patronage.

Angry caller: "Well, I feel a bit better that there *may* be something you can do about this. But frankly, I'm very disappointed in the service your company provides, and I don't think I'll recommend you to my friends."

Unhelpful response: "Well, if that's the way you feel, I'll go ahead and cancel your order and refund your money. We have enough other customers without having to worry about complainers like you!"

Helpful response: "I'm going to look into the computer file right now and see what I can do. Well, it looks like we mistyped your street address, after all. Most likely the package is being returned to us right now. Rather than wait to get that sweater back, I'll repeat the order and send it to you overnight at our expense. Sorry about the inconvenience—I do hope your daughter likes the gift!"

Your helpful response: _____

_____

_____

_____

_____

Exhibit F: Handling "No-Nonsense" Callers

Some callers are all business on the phone. They don't have time or interest in being "nice" on a business call. You can recognize this type of caller by his or her trademark gruffness and lack of social polish on the phone. This caller may talk to you twice a week but has never once asked you about your family or what you did on vacation. Although at first it may seem that this type of caller is trying to intimidate you, impose his or her authority, or show disapproval, there is another explanation for this no-nonsense telephone manner. Often, this type of caller sees the phone as *strictly* a business tool, to be used for business communication only, no frills or niceties required. The best way to respond to the no-nonsense caller is to match the caller's style and take cues from his or her formality on the phone. Once you understand that the caller is not being unfriendly or unkind for the sake of sheer unpleasantness, you will be able to respond calmly. In other words, don't take this type of caller's gruffness *personally*—it's just a phone style that needs a particular response. The following techniques help you match the caller's tone so you can get down to the business of your call:

1. Keep the conversation strictly business. The no-nonsense caller will be thrown off track if you try to get personal. Your job is to meet the caller on his or her level, and you'll need to forgo ''chit chat'' and pleasantries.

No-nonsense caller: ''Hello, Mr. Martinez. Listen, I want to talk to you about setting up the status meeting on Monday. What time do you plan to hold this meeting? I have my agenda already set up and I want to go over it with you and Ms. Muller. Let's meet today at 3:00 so we can walk through the status report.''

Inappropriate response: ''Hi, Sarah! What did you think of that office party last week? I thought things got out of hand a bit but everyone had a good time anyway. Oh, that meeting, let me see . . . Can I call you back later? I'm not quite ready mapping out my part of the meeting yet. Relax, it will go fine. Don't get so worked up, OK? I'll take care of it.''

Appropriate response: ''Hi, Ms. Wain. I'm glad you want to talk about that status meeting—this is important now because we want everyone to be on the same time-table for this project. We're on for Monday at 10:00. I'll talk to Ms. Muller and get conference room C for 3:00 today so we can discuss the Monday meeting. See you then.''

Your appropriate response: _____

_____

_____

_____

_____

_____

2. Don't take seemingly aggressive language personally. Remember that your caller probably doesn't intend to intimidate you. Make sure you remain calm and unflappable rather than responding defensively. This will likely diffuse aggression, or at the least it will give you control over the direction of the phone call.

No-nonsense caller: "Look, Mr. Martinez, I don't have time for fooling around here. I need you to take care of this now or both our jobs are on the line. Drop everything you're working on and make this your top priority! And I *don't* want to hear that you're taking a long lunch today—I need you at your desk and on full alert!"

Inappropriate response: "Sarah, I will not have you talk to me that way! Who do you think you are anyway? Do I have to remind you that we're team members here and that you're *not* my boss? Get off your high horse and solve the problem yourself—I'm not here to bail you out of your own problems. I'm going to lunch and I'll be back whenever I please, thank you very much!"

Appropriate response: "Now let's see if we can work together here. Why don't you come down to my desk and we can look at the problem together. I do have lunch plans, but I think we can get a grip on the problem before I go out. It sounds to me like it's similar to the issue we had on the Jarvis account last week. Let's check it out."

Your appropriate response: _____

_____

_____

_____

_____

_____

Exhibit G: The Caller Who Can't Hang Up

We all know people who can't seem to finish a phone call. These people talk and talk without working toward a resolution. Although this type of open-ended phone conversation may be fine for personal calls, it is often problematic during business calls since neither party can move on to other tasks and projects. The best way to handle never-ending calls is to take charge and actively direct the conversation toward closure. Take responsibility for moving the call along its course and then ending it when your business is completed. Use the following guidelines to help you handle the never-ending call.

1. Keep the conversation to the business at hand and resist being drawn into personal or unrelated conversation. This can be tricky when a chatty caller is particularly insistent on prolonging a phone call, but stick to your guns!

Chatty caller: "Yes, I can attend the meeting on Tuesday afternoon. Do you think Ray will be there? I want to ask him about his trip to Cancun and also whether he knows of any good travel agents I can talk to. Do you know any travel agents? Oh, you went to Florida on your last vacation, maybe you think I should go there instead? What do you think about the vacation policy in general? It seems to me . . .''

Inappropriate response: ''Well, Ray won't be there but I happen to know he uses Charter Travel. Personally, I prefer going through the Yellow Pages to get the cheapest deal. But then again, I'm new here and only get one week of paid vacation. It seems unfair to me and I really want to talk to my boss, but I'm afraid. I was thinking of maybe having a meeting with other new employees . . . ''

Appropriate response: ''OK, glad you can make it on Tuesday. Bring the minutes from the last meeting so we can refer to them. I can't talk right now; do you want to set up lunch some time this week?''

Your appropriate response: _____

_____

_____

_____

_____

_____

2. Take charge of ending the call. Be polite and courteous—you don't want the caller to feel that he or she is a nuisance. Just be firm and unbending. Remember that business calls are just that and shouldn't become long and drawn out beyond their intended purpose.

Chatty caller: ''So, I'll bring the minutes to the next meeting, but before you go, let me just ask you what you think about the boss's new policy on vacation time. I feel that she's taking advantage of entry-level people and shouldn't be allowed to get away with this! I've been to personnel and . . . ''

Inappropriate response: ''Yeah, it seems rather unfair to me, too. I was talking to Jan about it the other day and she said that I should just keep quiet or risk losing my job. It makes me feel a bit uneasy, I must say, and I want . . .''

Appropriate response: ''I know you're as busy as I am, so I'm going to let you go now. I'll talk to you after work. Bye.''

Your appropriate response: _____

_____

_____

_____

_____

_____

B Answers to Odd-Numbered Quick Quiz Questions

Chapter 1

1. The four main components of communication are: the speaker, the message, the channel, and the listener.

3. The three most common settings for business speaking are: one-on-one meetings, group meetings, and formal presentations.

5. A business meeting is a good place to show your strengths because with the right practice and training, you can be an effective business speaker and therefore a valued member of your organization.

7. Fear of speaking often interferes with career development.

9. Enthusiasm about speaking and communication will have positive effects on speakers and listeners alike.

Chapter 2

1. Some physical characteristics related to speaking fear are: perspiration, shaky hands or knees, rapid heartbeat, tightness in the chest, cracking voice, upset stomach, dry mouth, and shortness of breath.

3. One negative influence of television is that people try to imitate the speaking skills and styles of TV personalities.

5. Yes. Channels carry your message to the audience, and the better you understand and control these channels, the less nervous you'll be.

7. Some examples of positive self-talk include: "I have prepared well." "I will give the best speech I can." "My audience is interested in my topic and wants me to succeed."

9. Diaphragmatic breathing is appropriate for speaking.

Chapter 3

1. Improving your voice and your speech will help you all around — in and out of business-speaking situations.

3. Assimilation is the running together of sounds or words.

5. The eight plosive sounds are: b, d, g, j, p, t, k, ch.

7. Rate is the number of words spoken per minute. Pace is the space put between thoughts during speaking.

9. Speaking speed should always be varied throughout a speech to provide interest.

Chapter 4

1. People's speech patterns are usually either inductive or deductive.

3. The specific to general speech pattern is called *inductive*.

5. Using the numerical transition method will allow your audience to anticipate the points you will be making.

7. The speaker develops ideas in Step 3.

9. Step 3 should make up the longest part of your speech.

Chapter 5

1. The purpose of informative speaking is to carry an idea from one source to another.

3. Use the PPI questionnaire when you need to understand your audience.

5. Three guidelines for effective, informative business speaking are: be clear, be concise, and be consistent.

7. Some factors affecting ethos, pathos, and logos are: time of day, listener's age, listener's knowledge of subject, weather, setting, location, clothing, speaker's voice, vocabulary, relationship to listeners, previous experiences between speaker and listener, use of visual aids.

9. A mixed message occurs when a speaker says one thing but shows another.

Chapter 6

1. A meeting occurs any time two or more people exchange ideas.

3. The first step in the self-sell you would use in an interview is to make a can-do statement.

5. Step 2 in the problem-solving format is to define the terms.

7. In the problem-solving format, solutions are suggested in Step 4.

9. The term *hidden agenda* means that meeting participants are not being clear about the true purpose or intention of the meeting.

Chapter 7

1. The six Cs are: be clear, be concise, be consistent, be colorful, be concrete, and be correct.

3. If visuals and words don't match, your listeners will spend more time trying to decipher this inconsistency than they spend listening to you.

5. The words *I* and *me* should not act as substitutes for *myself*.

7. Color words are words spoken with special emphasis to bring liveliness, weight, emphasis, or meaning to a thought.

9. Construct your sentences consistently, concisely, and clearly when explaining complicated subjects.

Chapter 8

1. In business-speaking terms, your audio channel is everything you say, and your video channel is everything your audience sees.

3. You should pay careful attention to your clothing *and* your jewelry—both send messages about your seriousness.

5. A mixed message occurs when facial expression or body language contradict the spoken message.

7. Moving your eyes around the room in an X, Y, or Z pattern is a good, inclusive eye contact technique with a large group of people.

9. Constant gesturing is too distracting to the audience and makes the speaker seem nervous.

Chapter 9

1. Listening is paying active attention to the speaker—therefore, it is voluntary.

3. Most people spend about 55 percent of the workday listening.

5. Getting ready to listen means that you get physically prepared, use note-taking materials, and remove any distractions.

7. Paraphrasing gives you an important check on the accuracy of what you heard, and it lets the speaker know you were paying attention.

9. By learning to really pay attention, you develop the ability to identify and follow the theme, main points, and supporting points a speaker is making.

Chapter 10

1. Interruption. Ringing telephones at work should be thought of as opportunities to present your company's image to the public, *not* as interruptions to your work.
3. Image. When you are on the phone, you verbally project your company's image.
5. If you eat while on the phone, you run the risk of sounding disrespectful and unprofessional.
7. Be sure you know who you're calling, know why you're calling, and know about how long the call should be.
9. To ensure that your message won't fall through the cracks, ask your message taker's name and thank him or her for helping you.

Chapter 11

1. The three most commonly used visual aids in business speaking are overhead transparencies, slides, and flipcharts.
3. When using visual aids, you should always keep synchronization, introduction and setup, and the talk and do rules in mind.
5. Use the introduction technique described in the chapter just before showing each visual.
7. When using transparencies, leave the light on, rather than turning it off between each transparency.
9. By showing only one item per transparency, you'll ensure that your listeners pay attention to *your explanation* of that single thought or idea.

Index